Interactions Access
Integrated Skills

Robert Baldwin

Laurie Blass

Pamela Hartmann

James Mentel

John P. Nelson

Marilynn Spaventa

Emily Austin Thrush

Patricia K. Werner

High Beginning

 **McGraw-Hill
Contemporary**

McGraw-Hill/Contemporary

A Division of The McGraw·Hill Companies

Interactions Access Integrated Skills

Published by McGraw-Hill/Contemporary, a business unit of The McGraw-Hill Companies, Inc.,
1221 Avenue of the Americas, New York, NY 10020. Copyright © 2003 by The McGraw-Hill Companies, Inc.
All rights reserved. No part of this publication may be reproduced or distributed in any form or by any means,
or stored in a database or retrieval system, without the prior written consent of The McGraw-Hill Companies,
Inc., including, but not limited to, in any network or other electronic storage or transmission, or broadcast
for distance learning.

Some ancillaries, including electronic and print components, may not be available to customers
outside the United States.

This book is printed on recycled, acid-free paper containing 10% postconsumer waste.

2 3 4 5 6 7 8 9 0 QPD/QPD 0 9 8 7 6 5 4

ISBN 0-07-231393-5
ISBN 0-07-112436-5 (ISE)

Editorial director: *Tina B. Carver*
Development editor: *Annie Sullivan*
Director of marketing: *Thomas P. Dare*
Production manager: *Genevieve Kelley*
Interior designer: *Michael Warrell, Design Solutions*
Photo researcher: *Amelia Ames Hill Associates/Amy Bethea*
Compositor: *Point West, Inc.*
Typeface: *10.5/12 Times Roman*
Printer: *Quebecor World Dubuque*

The credits section for this book begins on page 260 and is considered an extension of
the copyright page.

INTERNATIONAL EDITION ISBN 0-07-112436-5
Copyright © 2003. Exclusive rights by The McGraw-Hill Companies, Inc., for manufacture and
export. This book cannot be re-exported from the country to which it is sold by McGraw-Hill.
The International Edition is not available in North America.

www.mhcontemporary.com/interactionsmosaic

Interactions Access
Integrated Skills

Interactions Access   **Integrated Skills**

Help your students achieve academic success!

Interactions Integrated Skills is a theme-based, three-level, four-skills ESL/EFL series designed to prepare students for academic content. Derived from the first three levels of the popular *Interactions Mosaic, 4th edition*, the series combines communicative activities with skill-building exercises in listening, speaking, reading, writing, and grammar to boost students' academic success.

Interactions Integrated Skills features:

- complete scope and sequence in the table of contents
- consistent chapter structure to aid in lesson planning
- placement tests and chapter quizzes in the instructor's manuals
- three videos of authentic news broadcasts to expand the chapter themes
- audio programs that include both the listening and reading selections
- additional practice and expansion opportunities on the Website

In This Chapter gives students a preview of the upcoming material.

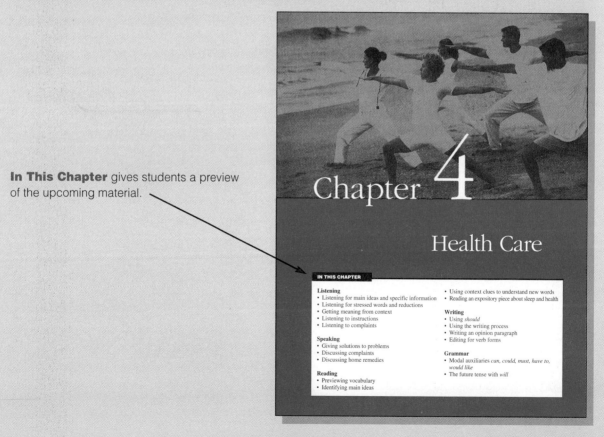

Chapter **4**

Health Care

IN THIS CHAPTER

Listening
- Listening for main ideas and specific information
- Listening for stressed words and reductions
- Getting meaning from context
- Listening to instructions
- Listening to complaints

Speaking
- Giving solutions to problems
- Discussing complaints
- Discussing home remedies

Reading
- Previewing vocabulary
- Identifying main ideas

- Using context clues to understand new words
- Reading an expository piece about sleep and health

Writing
- Using *should*
- Using the writing process
- Writing an opinion paragraph
- Editing for verb forms

Grammar
- Modal auxiliaries *can, could, must, have to, would like*
- The future tense with *will*

PART 1 Listening to Conversations

Before You Listen

1 Preparing to Listen. Look at these photos.

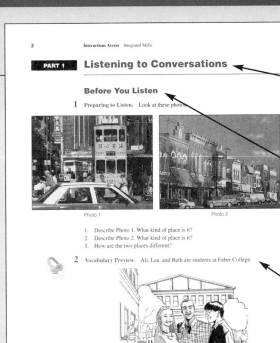

Photo 1   Photo 2

1. Describe Photo 1. What kind of place is it?
2. Describe Photo 2. What kind of place is it?
3. How are the two places different?

2 Vocabulary Preview. Ali, Lee, and Beth are students at Faber College.

Part 1 Listening to Conversations
presents an introductory conversation
and focuses on the rhythm and intonation
of natural language through stress and
reduction activities.

**Before You Listen, Listen, and After
You Listen** sections activate students' prior
knowledge, guide them to listen for main
ideas and specific information, and reinforce
their understanding through comprehension
questions and a vocabulary review.

Vocabulary Preview allows students to
anticipate new vocabulary in the listening and
reading selections.

PART 2 Listening Skills

Getting Meaning from Context

1 Vocabulary Preview.   You are going
to hear some conversations about
food. Listen to these words and
expressions from the conversations.
Circle the ones you don't know.

Nouns	Verb
charge	to beat
teaspoon	
onion soup	
carrot	
cucumber	
produce	
ounce	

2 Using Context Clues.

1. Listen to the first part of each conversation.
2. Listen to the question and circle the letter of the best answer.
3. Then listen to the last part to hear the correct answer.

1. Where are Lee and Alicia?
   a. in a restaurant   b. in a supermarket   c. in a cafeteria

2. What's Lee asking about?
   a. the waiter   b. the menu   c. the bill

3. What are David and Beth doing?
   a. cooking something
   b. shopping
   c. eating in a restaurant

4. Where are Ali and Alicia?
   a. at a restaurant
   b. at a produce stand (a small fruit and vegetable market)
   c. in a supermarket produce (fruit and vegetable) section

5. Which spaghetti sauce is the best buy?
   a. the spaghetti sauce with mushrooms
   b. the eight-ounce size for $1.06
   c. the size for 99 cents

Part 2 Listening Skills increases
students' listening comprehension through
task-based practice.

Photos and illustrations provide
valuable context for the chapter topic.

Using Context Clues practices test-taking
strategies vital for success on standardized
tests.

D   26 percent of women between age thirty and thirty-four live alone, and more
      than 27 percent of men of the same age live alone.
          There are also big changes in Quebec, Canada. In 1965, a traditional
      family was important. Almost 90 percent of men and 93.5 percent of women
      were married. But in 1985, only 49 percent of men and 51.7 percent of women
      were married! Now more than one-third (⅓) of all babies have parents that
      are not married. More than one-third of all marriages end in divorce.
E   There are many new types of families. The world is changing, and families
      are changing too.

After You Read

4 Finding the Main Ideas. Circle a letter for each blank.

1. The main idea is that _____ .
    a. in North Africa, families are big, but in Europe, they're small
    b. families around the world are changing
    c. ⅓ of all marriages end in divorce

2. The writer thinks that new families are _____ .
    a. good because they are small
    b. different from families in the past
    c. bad because people don't live together

5 Understanding Pronouns. Find and circle the meaning of each underlined pronoun.
Then draw an arrow from the pronoun to its meaning.

1. (Fifty to a hundred people) live together in a group of houses. These are all
    family members.

2. Men and women spend a lot of time at work. They don't spend a lot of time
    together as a family.

3. They don't spend a lot of time together as a family. This can be very difficult.

4. More and more countries are recognizing gay partnerships and marriages.
    For example, Denmark, Sweden, Norway, the Netherlands, Hungary, and the U.S.
    state of Vermont all recognize these as legal unions.

Discussing the Reading

6 Talk about your answers to these questions with your classmates.

1. What kind of family do you live in?
2. Why are families in some countries smaller than in the past?
3. Why are there more single-parent families now?

Before You Read, Read, and After You Read sections provide scaffolding to help students understand authentic language, identify main ideas, and reinforce their understanding through comprehension questions.

Language-learning strategies such as making good guesses, understanding pronouns, and using visual graphics provide students with reading comprehension tools.

Discussing the Reading encourages students to contribute their own opinions on high-interest subjects related to the readings.

Practicing the Writing Process

1 Exploring Ideas: Brainstorming and Free Writing. You are going to write
an opinion paragraph that answers this question: Should tobacco be illegal (against
the law)? Sometimes you can get ideas by brainstorming on your own, for example,
when you freewrite. Other times it's good to work with a group or the whole class
and get ideas together. In a group or as a class, make a list of reasons tobacco should
be made illegal and reasons tobacco shouldn't be made illegal. On separate paper,
write down ideas for both sides of the argument.

Now decide which side you are on. Think about your argument and freewrite your
ideas. Work with a partner. Read aloud your ideas. Then discuss them with your
partner.

2 Writing the First Draft. Write a first draft of your paragraph. Begin with
"This country should make tobacco illegal" or "This country shouldn't make tobacco
illegal." When necessary, use modals from the list on page 80.

3 Editing. Check your opinion paragraph. Use the following checklist to correct
any mistakes.

Editing Checklist

1. Are the verbs used with modals in the simple form (*study, work, discover, go*)?
2. Are the modals correct (*should* if you think something is a good idea or the
    correct thing to do, *will* if you believe something is definitely going to
    happen in the future, etc.)?
3. Do your sentences begin with capital letters?
4. Do other words in the writing need capital letters?
5. Do your sentences end with periods?

4 Peer Editing. Show your paragraph to another student. Read each other's paragraphs.
Does your partner's paragraph have a topic sentence, interesting reasons and
explanations, a conclusion? Use the Editing Checklist to check your classmate's
paragraph.

5 Writing the Second Draft. Write your second draft and give it to your teacher.

Practicing the Writing Process encourages thoughtful composition by guiding students step by step from exploring topics to self-editing.

Groupwork maximizes opportunities for discussion and negotiation.

Editing Checklists guide students in learning the editing process.

Peer Editing encourages students to share their writing and to provide constructive feedback to their classmates.

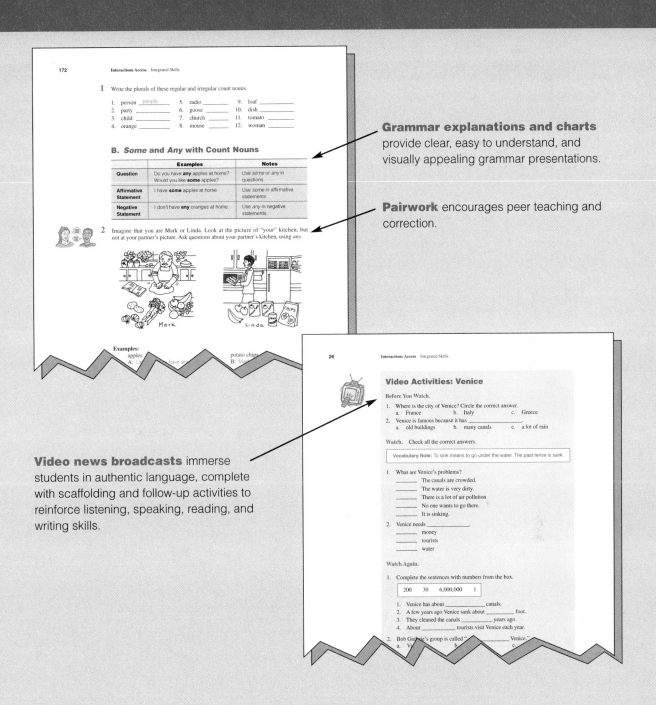

172 Interactions Access Integrated Skills

1 Write the plurals of these regular and irregular count nouns.

1. person _people_
2. party _____
3. child _____
4. orange _____
5. radio _____
6. goose _____
7. church _____
8. mouse _____
9. loaf _____
10. dish _____
11. tomato _____
12. woman _____

B. *Some* and *Any* with Count Nouns

	Examples	Notes
Question	Do you have **any** apples at home? Would you like **some** apples?	Use *some* or *any* in questions.
Affirmative Statement	I have **some** apples at home.	Use *some* in affirmative statements.
Negative Statement	I don't have **any** oranges at home.	Use *any* in negative statements.

2 Imagine that you are Mark or Linda. Look at the picture of "your" kitchen, but not at your partner's picture. Ask questions about your partner's kitchen, using *any*.

Mark   Linda

Examples:
apples   potato chips
A: Li... ...have an...   B: Ma...

Grammar explanations and charts provide clear, easy to understand, and visually appealing grammar presentations.

Pairwork encourages peer teaching and correction.

Video news broadcasts immerse students in authentic language, complete with scaffolding and follow-up activities to reinforce listening, speaking, reading, and writing skills.

26 Interactions Access Integrated Skills

Video Activities: Venice

Before You Watch.

1. Where is the city of Venice? Circle the correct answer.
   a. France   b. Italy   c. Greece
2. Venice is famous because it has _____.
   a. old buildings   b. many canals   c. a lot of rain

Watch. Check all the correct answers.

> **Vocabulary Note:** To sink means to go under the water. The past tense is sank

1. What are Venice's problems?
   _____ The canals are crowded.
   _____ The water is very dirty.
   _____ There is a lot of air pollution
   _____ No one wants to go there.
   _____ It is sinking.
2. Venice needs _____.
   _____ money
   _____ tourists
   _____ water

Watch Again.

1. Complete the sentences with numbers from the box.

   | 200 | 30 | 6,000,000 | 1 |

   1. Venice has about _____ canals.
   2. A few years ago Venice sank about _____ foot.
   3. They cleaned the canals _____ years ago.
   4. About _____ tourists visit Venice each year.

2. Bob Gut...ie's group is called "_____ Venice."
   a. Vi...   b. ...   c. ...

➤ Don't forget to check out the new *Interactions Integrated Skills* Website at www.mhcontemporary.com/interactionsmosaic. It provides additional practice, interactive activities, and links to student and teacher resources.

Interactions Access Integrated Skills

Chapter	Listening Skills / Tasks	Speaking Tasks / Skills	Reading Type & Topic
1 Neighborhoods, Cities, and Towns **Page 1**	■ Listening for main ideas ■ Listening for specific information ■ Listening for stressed words and reductions ■ Getting meaning from context ■ Listening for time and distance ■ Listening for fares	■ Role-playing personal information ■ Talking about transportation	■ Exposition (cities)
2 Shopping and e-Commerce **Page 27**	■ Listening for main ideas ■ Listening for specific information ■ Listening for stressed words and reductions ■ Getting meaning from context ■ Listening for prices ■ Listening for store names ■ Listening to online shopping information	■ Asking and answering questions about shopping habits ■ Comparing prices and stores	■ Exposition (online shopping)
3 Friends and Family **Page 49**	■ Listening for main ideas ■ Listening for specific information ■ Listening for stressed words and reductions ■ Getting meaning from context ■ Listening to voicemail messages ■ Listening to descriptions of people	■ Talking about staying in touch with family members ■ Discussing appearance	■ Exposition (family structures)
4 Health Care **Page 69**	■ Listening for main ideas ■ Listening for specific information ■ Listening for stressed words and reductions ■ Getting meaning from context ■ Listening to instructions ■ Listening to complaints	■ Giving solutions to problems ■ Discussing complaints ■ Discussing home remedies	■ Exposition (sleep and health)
5 Men and Women **Page 89**	■ Listening for main ideas ■ Listening for specific information ■ Listening for stressed words and reductions ■ Getting meaning from context ■ Listening to invitations ■ Listening to responses	■ Talking about dating ■ Discussing invitations	■ Exposition (men's and women's language)

Reading Skills / Strategies	Writing & Editing Skills	Grammar	Video Topics
■ Previewing vocabulary ■ Identifying main ideas ■ Making inferences about figurative language	■ Using *there is/there are* ■ Using *to be* + complement ■ Understanding the writing process ■ Writing a descriptive paragraph ■ Editing for capitalization and punctuation	■ The present tense of *be* ■ *It* with weather and time expressions ■ *There is/there are* ■ Prepositions of time and place	■ Venice
■ Previewing vocabulary ■ Using context clues to understand new words ■ Understanding *going to* for the future ■ Understanding irregular past tense verbs ■ Identifying main ideas ■ Using the organization of an information article	■ Using transitive and intransitive verbs ■ Using the writing process ■ Writing about future predictions ■ Editing for spelling, capitalization, and punctuation	■ The present continuous tense ■ Prepositions of place	■ Online Pharmacies
■ Previewing vocabulary ■ Identifying main ideas ■ Using context clues to understand new words ■ Understanding pronouns	■ Using the simple present tense ■ Using the writing process ■ Writing a personal letter ■ Editing for specific information	■ The simple present tense ■ Adverbs of frequency ■ The simple present versus the present continuous	■ Pet Behavior
■ Previewing vocabulary ■ Identifying main ideas ■ Using context clues to understand new words	■ Using *should* ■ Using the writing process ■ Writing an opinion paragraph ■ Editing for verb forms	■ Modal auxiliaries *can, could, must, have to, would like* ■ The future tense with *will*	■ Brain Surgery
■ Previewing vocabulary ■ Identifying main ideas ■ Using context clues to understand new words ■ Identifying the best synopsis	■ Using direct and indirect objects ■ Using the writing process ■ Writing a narrative ■ Editing for use of object pronouns, verb tense, interest, and capitalization and punctuation	■ The simple past tense with *be* and regular verbs	■ Women's Football

Chapter	Listening Skills / Tasks	Speaking Tasks / Skills	Reading Type & Topic
6 Sleep and Dreams **Page 111**	■ Listening for main ideas ■ Listening for specific information ■ Listening for stressed words and reductions ■ Getting meaning from context ■ Listening to a lecture ■ Listening for test scores ■ Listening to a dream	■ Pronouncing teens and tens ■ Talking about sleep and dreams ■ Discussing a lecture ■ Retelling a dream	■ Exposition (sleep and dreams)
7 Work and Lifestyles **Page 135**	■ Listening for main ideas ■ Listening for specific information ■ Listening for stressed words and reductions ■ Getting meaning from context ■ Listening to job interviews ■ Listening to future plans	■ Pronouncing college majors and job titles ■ Asking about personal characteristics related to jobs ■ Discussing job interviews	■ Exposition (volunteerism)
8 Food and Nutrition **Page 157**	■ Listening for main ideas ■ Listening for specific information ■ Listening for stressed words and reductions ■ Getting meaning from context ■ Listening to job instructions ■ Following recipes	■ Talking about healthy and unhealthy foods ■ Naming foods ■ Discussing opinions about food	■ Exposition (diets)
9 Great Destinations **Page 177**	■ Listening for main ideas ■ Listening for specific information ■ Listening for stressed words and reductions ■ Getting meaning from context ■ Listening for places on a map ■ Listening to a tour guide ■ Listening for flight information	■ Describing vacation destinations ■ Discussing flight information	■ Exposition (vacations)
10 Our Planet **Page 199**	■ Listening for main ideas ■ Listening for specific information ■ Listening for stressed words and reductions ■ Getting meaning from context ■ Listening to persuasive messages	■ Identifying information requested through emphasized words in a question	■ Exposition (the greenhouse effect)

Reading Skills / Strategies	Writing & Editing Skills	Grammar	Video Topics
■ Previewing vocabulary ■ Identifying main ideas ■ Using context clues to understand new words ■ Recognizing words with similar meaning	■ Using gerunds and infinitives after verbs ■ Using linking verbs ■ Using the writing process ■ Writing a narrative ■ Editing for complete sentences and capitalization and punctuation	■ The simple past tense with irregular verbs ■ Using *too* and *either* with short statements ■ *Used to* for past habitual actions or situations	■ Children and Sleep
■ Previewing vocabulary ■ Identifying main ideas ■ Using context clues to understand new words ■ Inferring the author's point of view	■ Using past tense verbs ■ Using the writing process ■ Writing an experience narrative ■ Editing for verb forms, complete sentences, and capitalization and punctuation	■ The past continuous tense ■ The past continuous versus the simple past	■ Dentist Fashion Designer
■ Previewing vocabulary ■ Identifying main ideas ■ Using context clues to understand new words ■ Recognizing opposites	■ Using the command form of verbs ■ Using the writing process ■ Writing directions on how to do something ■ Editing for sequence words, verb forms, and capitalization and punctuation	■ Count and noncount nouns ■ *Some* and *any* with count and noncount nouns ■ Counting units ■ Questions with *How many/how much*	■ Diets
■ Previewing vocabulary ■ Identifying main ideas ■ Using context clues to understand new words	■ Using predicate adjectives ■ Using the writing process ■ Writing a postcard or short letter ■ Editing for verb tense, complete sentences, and capitalization and punctuation	■ Adjectives with *–ing* and *–ed* ■ Comparative adjectives ■ Superlatives with adjectives and adverbs	■ Cancun
■ Previewing vocabulary ■ Identifying main ideas ■ Identifying specific information ■ Using context clues to understand new words ■ Drawing conclusions	■ Analyzing a composition ■ Using the writing process ■ Writing a problem/ solution composition ■ Editing for composition development, verb forms, capitalization and punctuation, and spelling	■ Regular and irregular past participles ■ The present perfect tense ■ The passive voice with simple tenses	■ Recycling

Chapter 1

Neighborhoods, Cities, and Towns

PART 1   Listening to Conversations

Before You Listen

1 **Preparing to Listen.**   Look at these photos.

Photo 1

Photo 2

1. Describe Photo 1. What kind of place is it?
2. Describe Photo 2. What kind of place is it?
3. How are the two places different?

2 **Vocabulary Preview.**   Ali, Lee, and Beth are students at Faber College.

1. Listen to these words from their conversation. Circle the ones you don't know.

   Nouns   **Adjective**
   capital   interesting
   hometown
   population
   transportation

2. Guess the meanings of the underlined words. Write your guess on the lines. Check your answers with a dictionary or your teacher.

   1. Life in a big city is always <u>interesting</u>; it's never dull.
      My guess: _____
   2. What kind of <u>transportation</u> do you use—the train, the bus, or the subway?
      My guess: _____
   3. My <u>hometown</u> is Mexico City. I was born there and I still live there.
      My guess: _____
   4. Paris is the <u>capital</u> of France. The government offices are there.
      My guess: _____
   5. Seoul, Korea has a large <u>population</u>: more than thirteen million people live there.
      My guess: _____

Listen

3 **Listening for Main Ideas.** Listen to the conversation. As you listen, answer these questions.

1. Where is Lee from?
2. Is Lee from a small town?
3. Where is Beth from?
4. Is Beth from a small town?

4 **Listening for Specific Information.** Listen again. Circle the letter of the best answer to each question.

1. What two greetings do you hear in the conversation? (Circle two.)
   a. How are things?   b. Hi!   c. How's it going?

2. Ali introduces Lee to Beth. What does he say?
   a. Beth, this is Lee.
   b. Beth, please meet my friend Lee.
   c. Beth, this is my friend, Lee.

3. What is Lee's answer?
   a. Nice meeting you.   b. Nice to meet you.   c. Hi!

After You Listen

5   **Understanding Main Ideas.**   Circle the letter of the correct answer.

1. Who is Beth?
   a. Lee's cousin.
   b. Ali's friend.
   c. Ali's cousin.

2. What does Lee say about Seoul?
   a. It has a good library.
   b. It has good public transportation.
   c. It has about 20,000 people.

3. What does Beth say about San Anselmo?
   a. It's a big city.
   b. It's the capital of California.
   c. It has about 20,000 people.

6   **Vocabulary Review.**   Complete these sentences. Use words from the list.

capital	interesting	
hometown	population	transportation

1. Seoul is the _____ of Korea.
2. There's good public _____ in Seoul.
3. What's the _____ of Seoul? Over thirteen million people live there.
4. What's your _____? I'm from San Anselmo, California.
5. Are your classes _____?

Stress

Important words are stressed in English. That is, we say them louder and clearer than other words.

Nice	to	**meet**	you.
Important	Not important	Important	Not important

7 **Listening for Stressed Words.** Listen to the first part of the conversation again. The <u>underlined</u> words are stressed.

Ali: <u>Beth</u>! Hey, <u>Beth</u>! <u>How's</u> it <u>going</u>?
Beth: <u>Ali</u>! Hi! I'm <u>fine</u>. How're <u>you</u>?
Ali: <u>Fine</u>, thanks. <u>Beth</u>, this is <u>Lee</u>. Lee, this is my <u>friend</u>, <u>Beth</u>.
Lee: <u>Nice</u> to <u>meet</u> you.
Beth: Nice to meet <u>you</u>. Are you from around <u>here</u>?
Lee: <u>No</u>. I'm from <u>Seoul</u>, Korea.
Beth: Oh, that's <u>interesting</u>. <u>Seoul's</u> the <u>capital</u> of Korea, <u>isn't</u> it?
Lee: <u>Yes</u>, that's <u>right</u>. How about <u>you</u>? What's <u>your</u> <u>hometown</u>?

Contractions

Contractions are a way to combine words. When you put the two words together, you drop letters and replace them with an apostrophe ('). People use them in speaking and in writing.

Long Form	**Contraction**
I am from Seoul.	I'm from Seoul.

8 **Comparing Long Forms and Contractions.** Listen to the following sentences from the conversation. They contain contractions. Repeat them after the speaker.

Long Form	**Contraction**
1. How is it going?	How's it going?
2. I am fine.	I'm fine.
3. How are you?	How're you?
4. Seoul is the capital.	Seoul's the capital.
5. It is a really big city.	It's a really big city.
6. That is a lot of people!	That's a lot of people!
7. There is good public transportation.	There's good public transportation.

9 **Listening for Contractions.** Listen to the sentences. Circle the letter of the sentence that you hear.

1. a. I'm fine.   b. I am fine.
2. a. He is from Seoul.   b. He's from Seoul.
3. a. It is the capital of Korea. b. It's the capital of Korea.
4. a. There are many people there. b. There're many people there.
5. a. What's the population? b. What is the population?

Talk It Over

1. Work in groups of four. Each person in the group should choose a role-play card and read the information on the card. You are going to answer questions about the character on your card.

2. Write the names of your group members in the spaces at the top of the chart.

3. Look at the example (Stacy). Practice asking your teacher the questions and write his/her answers on the chart.

   Example: What's your name?   Where are you from?
                   Stacy.   I'm from Ottawa.

4. Ask your group members the questions. Write their answers on the chart. Answer their questions using the information on your character card.

What's your Name	_Stacy_	Teacher _____	Name _____	Name _____	Name _____
1. Where are you from?	Ottawa				
2. Where's that?	Canada				
3. Is your hometown small, medium-sized, or big?	Medium-sized				
4. What's the population?	313,987				
5. Is there good public transportation?	Yes				
6. Your question:					

1.
City: Kyoto
Country: Japan
Small, medium-sized, or big? Big
Population: 1,461,140
Public Transportation: Yes

2.
City: Curitiba
Country: Brazil
Small, medium-sized, or big? Big
Population: 1,465,698
Public Transportation: Yes

3.
City: Puebla
Country: Mexico
Small, medium-sized, or big? Big
Population: 4,126,101
Public Transportation: Yes

4.
City: Chiang Mai
Country: Thailand
Small, medium-sized, or big? Medium-sized
Population: 164,902
Public Transportation: Yes

PART 2   Listening Skills

Getting Meaning from Context

1 Using Context Clues.

1. Listen to the first part of each conversation.
2. Listen to the question and circle the letter of the best answer.
3. Then listen to the last part to hear the correct answer.

1. What is Mexico City like?
   a. a town
   b. a city
   c. a very large city

2. Why isn't Lee going home for New Year's?
   a. because Seoul is far away
   b. because the airfare is cheap
   c. because the airfare costs too much money

3. How will the man go to Central Avenue?
   a. He'll go by bus.
   b. He'll walk.
   c. He'll go by car.

4. Why doesn't Beth take the subway?
   a. It's too crowded.
   b. It's not fast enough.
   c. It's too comfortable.

5. What does Ali like about his new place to live?
   a. It's small.
   b. It's cold.
   c. It's close to the school.

Listening for Time and Distance

Before You Listen

2 Preparing to Listen.   Before you listen, answer this question with a partner.

How do you get to school or work?

3   **Vocabulary Preview.**   Listen to these time and distance words. Circle the ones you don't know.

Time

a minute	two minutes	a two-minute ride/walk
an hour	two hours	a two-hour ride/walk
	half an hour	a half-hour ride/walk

Distance

a mile	two miles	a two-mile ride/walk

Listen

4   **Listening for Main Ideas.**   As you listen, answer these questions about the conversation.

1.   How does the man get to school?
2.   How does the woman get to school?

5   **Listening for Time and Distance.**   Listen again. Complete the conversation with words from the list.

one mile	ten miles	three-hour
thirty minutes	fifteen-minute	

Woman: So, how do you get to school every day?

Man: I take the subway.

Woman: You don't take the bus?

Man: Nah, the bus's too slow. It takes _____ to get to school
                from my place.
                                              1

Woman: Yeah, that's right…your place is far from the university.

Man: How about you?

Woman: Oh, I walk—my apartment's close—about _____ from
                                                                                    2
                school. It's just a _____ walk.
                                          3

Man: Wow, that's great. My place is far from school — about _____.
                                                                                          4
                So I *can't* walk.

Woman: Yeah, that's about a _____ walk!
                                              5

After You Listen

6   **Discussing Time and Distance.**   Talk in small groups about the answers to these questions.

1.   How far is school from your home?
2.   What is the best way to get to school?

Listening for Fares

Public Transportation in Vancouver

A Vancouver bus

The Sky Train elevated railway

A ferry

The West Coast Express train

Before You Listen

7   **Preparing to Listen.**   Before you listen, discuss this question with a partner.

What kinds of public transportation do you have in your town or city?
Check (✔) them.

_____ bus   _____ elevated railway

_____ subway   _____ train

_____ ferry   _____ other: _____

8   **Vocabulary Preview.**   Listen to these words and expressions about fares. Circle the ones you don't know.

Nouns		**Verbs**	**Expressions**
fare	seniors	be divided	in advance
exact change	ticket	be good for	
pass	zone		
public transportation			

Listen

9   **Listening for the Main Idea.**   Now listen to the information about public transportation in Vancouver, Canada. As you listen, try to answer this question:

What kinds of public transportation are there in Vancouver? Check (✔) them.

_____ bus   _____ elevated railway

_____ subway   _____ train

_____ ferry   _____ other: _____

10   **Listening for Fares.**

1.   Listen again and complete the chart with the zone prices.

Zones	Adults	Seniors, Students, and Children
Zone 1		
Zone 2		
Zone 3		

2.   Listen a third time. This time, listen for the special prices and the day pass prices.

   1.   Evenings, weekends, and holidays: _____

   2.   Day pass for adults: _____

   3.   Day pass for children: _____

After You Listen

11   **Discussing Transportation Information.**   Answer these questions in small groups:

1.   Do you have transportation zones in your city or town?
2.   Do you have special fares for seniors? For children? For students?
3.   Which kind of public transportation do you like best? Why?

| **PART 3** | # Reading |

Before You Read

1 Discuss the answers to these questions with a partner or in small groups.

   1.   Is this city large or small? Is it nice?

   2.   What is the problem with this city?

   3.   Do you like cities?

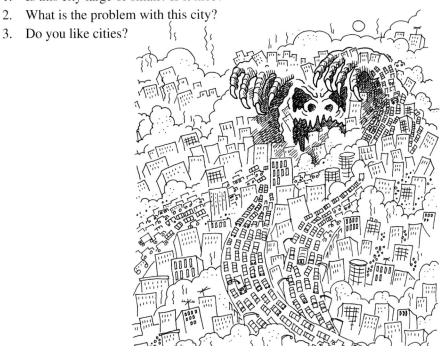

2 **Vocabulary Preview.**   It is not always necessary to use a dictionary to find the meaning of a word. Sometimes the meaning is after the word *is* or *are* in the sentence.

Example:

<u>Population</u> is the number of people in a city or country.

What is population? *the number of people in a city or country*

Answer the questions.

   1.   A <u>monster</u> is a big, terrible thing.

      What is a monster? _____

   2.   A <u>megacity</u> is a very, very large city.

      What is a megacity? _____

   3.   <u>Density</u> is the number of people in a square mile.

      What is density? _____

Read

3 Read the following article quickly. Then do the exercises.

___

Monster Cities

A | Are big cities wonderful places? Are they terrible? There are different ideas about this. William H. Whyte writes books about cities. He is happy in a crowded city. He loves busy streets with many stores and many people. He likes the life in city parks and restaurants.

B | Many people don't like big cities. They see the large population of cities, and they are afraid. Many cities are growing very fast. They are "monster" cities. (A monster is a big, terrible thing.) In some countries, there aren't jobs in small towns. People go to cities to work; 300,000 people go to Sao Paulo, Brazil, every year. These cities are megalopolises. A megalopolis is a very large city. But now there is a new word in English—megacity. A megacity is a very, very large city. Mexico City is a megacity with a population of more than 20,000,000. Tokyo-Yokohama is another megacity, with almost 30,000,000 people.

C | There are problems in all cities. There are big problems in a megalopolis or megacity. In U.S. cities, there are many people with no jobs and no homes. The air is dirty. There are too many cars. A terrible problem is crime. Many people are afraid of crime.

D | Population density is a big problem in megacities. Density is the number of people in an average square mile. In Seoul, South Korea, there are 45,953 people per square mile. Is this crowded? Yes! But in Teheran, Iran, there are 79,594 per square mile. Do you think William H. Whyte likes Hong Kong? The population density there is 247,004!

___

After You Read

4 **Finding the Main Ideas.**   Complete the sentences. Circle a letter for each blank.

1. "Monster Cities" is about ____.

    a.   the large number of small cities
    b.   the number of people in U.S. cities
    c.   the problems of megacities

2. Mexico City, Teheran, and Hong Kong are three ____.

    a.   small cities
    b.   very big, crowded cities
    c.   cities with no crime or dirty air

5 **Making Good Guesses.**   Circle the letter to complete the sentence.

The word *monster* is in the title ("Monster Cities") because ____.

a.   the writer is happy in big cities
b.   some cities are growing too fast
c.   there are people with no jobs and no homes

Discussing the Reading

6 Read the population chart with a partner. Then answer the questions together.

Population of Large Cities			
City, Country	**1995**	**2000**	**density***
Tokyo-Yokohama, Japan	28,447,000	29,971,000	24,463
Mexico City, Mexico	23,913,000	27,872,000	37,314
São Paulo, Brazil	21,539,000	25,354,000	38,528
Seoul, South Korea	19,065,000	21,976,000	45,953
New York, USA	14,638,000	14,648,000	11,473
Teheran, Iran	11,681,000	14,251,000	79,594
Jakarta, Indonesia	11,151,000	12,804,000	122,033
Los Angeles, USA	10,414,000	10,714,000	8,985
Hong Kong	5,841,000	5,956,000	247,004
*Population per square mile			

1. What is the population of Tokyo-Yokohama?

2. What is the population of São Paulo, Brazil?

3. What is the population of Mexico City?

4. What is the population density of Los Angeles, USA?

5. What is the population density of Seoul, South Korea?

6. What is the population density of Teheran, Iran?

7. What is the population density of Hong Kong?

8. What is the population of Hong Kong?

9. What is the population density of Jakarta, Indonesia?

Is your city large or small? What is the population? What is nice about your city?
What is a problem in your city? Do you like your city? Why or why not?

PART 4

Writing

Read this student's description of a favorite place.

> My Favorite Place
>
> I live in Los Angeles. My favorite place is near there. The name of the place is the Huntington Library and Gardens. There are many different kinds of gardens there. There is a Japanese garden, a desert garden, a rose garden, an Australian garden, and many others. My favorite garden is the rose garden.
>
> There are almost 1500 kinds of rose bushes in the garden. In the summer, many of them have flowers. There are roses from the 1600's to modern times, and there are red roses, pink roses, and roses of every other color. The garden is full of the smell of roses. The grass is very soft and green. Sometimes there is the sound of the big bell in the Japanese garden and there are always the sounds of birds and trees.
>
> The garden is a beautiful place.

Using Sentence Patterns

Sentence Pattern 1.   When we describe a place, we use basic sentence patterns over and over. One uses *there is/are* in this way.

there is / there are	+	noun phrase	+	prepositional phrase (optional)
There is		a rose bush		in the garden.

Good descriptions always have details. Details are specific facts. General statements are often boring. Details are interesting.

General Statement	**Detail or Fact**
There are many kinds of roses in the garden.	There are almost 1500 different kinds of rose bushes in the garden.
There are nice sounds.	There are always the sounds of the birds and the leaves in the trees.

Look at the student's description of the Huntington Gardens on page 14. Complete this chart using sentences from the description.

There is / There are	Noun Phrase	Adverb or Prepositional Phrase
There are	many different kinds of gardens	there.
	a Japanese garden, a desert garden, a rose garden, an Australian garden, and many others.	X
		in the garden.
There are		X
	red roses, pink roses, and roses of every other color.	X
		in the Japanese garden
There are always		X

Sentence Pattern 2.   The verb *to be* is often followed by complements.

> subject   +   be   +   complement
> I   am   from Japan.
>
> Sometimes the complement is a prepositional phrase.
>
> A lot of my neighbors   are   from different countries.
>
> Sometimes the complement is an adjective (a word that describes the subject).
>
> The stores   are   busy.
> The grass   is   very soft and green.

A paragraph is a group of sentences. The sentences are about the same idea. A paragraph always begins with an indented space. Read this paragraph and complete the chart.

indented space → I am a student. I live in Los Angeles. My favorite place is near there. The name of the place is the Huntington Library and Gardens. The library is a beautiful white building. In spring the gardens are full of flowers.

subject	be	complement
I	am	a student.
	is	near there.
The name of the place		
		a beautiful white building.
In spring the gardens		

Practicing the Writing Process

1 **Exploring Ideas: Brainstorming.**   Write six sentences about your favorite place. Use *there is* or *there are*. Then tell your group about the place but don't read your sentences.

1. There is / are _____.

2. _____.

3. _____.

4. _____.

5. _____.

6. _____.

2 **Writing the First Draft.**   A draft is when you practice or try writing something. Write a paragraph about your favorite place. Use Sentence Patterns 1 and 2.

3 **Editing.**   Good writers never write only one draft. They write, then edit (correct their work and make changes), then write at least a second draft. (Some writers write five or ten drafts!) Following are some things to look for when you edit.

Using Capital Letters and Correct Punctuation

■ Every sentence begins with a capital letter and ends with a period, exclamation mark, or question mark.

This is my neighborhood.
  ^   ^
capital   period

■ There is a comma between a city and state or a city and country.
San Francisco, California
Jakarta, Indonesia
     ^
   comma

■ These words have a capital letter.

names of cities	São Paulo
names of states	Texas
names of countries	Iran
person or thing from a country	American, Korean
languages	Japanese
street names	Olive Street, Sycamore Avenue
people's names	Etsuko Sasaki
names of stores, buildings, and parks	Han's Drugstore
the word "I"	

Now check the first draft of your paragraph about your favorite place. Use the following checklist to correct any mistakes.

Editing Checklist

1. Do your sentences begin with capital letters?
2. Do other words in your paragraph need capital letters?
3. Do your sentences end with periods?
4. Do any words in your paragraph need a comma between them?

 **4** **Peer Editing.**   Show your paragraph to another student. Read each other's paragraphs and discuss each other's work. Are there interesting details? Are the descriptions clear? Use the editing list to check your classmate's paragraph.

5 **Writing the Second Draft.**   Now you are ready to write your second draft. When you are finished, give it to your teacher.

PART 5

Grammar

A. Present Tense of *Be*: Affirmative Statements

Affirmative	Contracted Forms	
I **am** Japanese.	**I'm**	
He / She / It **is** in New York.	**He's / She's / It's**	Japanese.
You / We / They **are** students.	**You're / We're / They're**	

1 Use the correct form of the verb *be* and *I, you, she, he, we,* or *they* to complete these sentences.

1. Mariko ___is___ from Japan. ___She___ ___is___ Japanese.
2. Elizabeth _____ from Germany. _____ _____ German.
3. Carlos and Gabriel _____ from Mexico. _____ _____ Mexican.
4. I _____ from France. _____ _____ French.
5. Mr. Park _____ from Korea. _____ _____ Korean.
6. Hassan and I _____ from Syria. _____ _____ Syrian.
7. You _____ from Colombia. _____ _____ Colombian.
8. Carolina and Andre _____ from Brazil. _____ _____ Brazilian.

2 Read this paragraph. Write it again with contractions on your own paper.

Example: Hi, I'm Carlos...

Hi! I am Carlos, and I am from Mexico. I am a student in Chicago, but I am in New York on a tour. My brother Gabriel is here in New York too. He is on vacation. We are very excited about our trip. New York is wonderful! It is big, crowded, and interesting. Some people on our tour are afraid of the city. They are nervous—especially Mariko, an exchange student from Japan. She is very nice, but she is always lost and confused. Not Gabriel and me! We are in love with New York!

B. Present Tense of *Be*: Yes / No Questions

Singular	Plural
Am I happy? **Is** she / he / it lost?	**Are** you / we / they nervous?

3 Work with a partner. Ask and answer these questions. Answer using *Yes* or *No*.

Example: A: Is Mariko Japanese?   A: Is Carlos Japanese?
          B: Yes.   B: No.

1. Is Mariko in New York City now?
2. Is she from Hong Kong?
3. Is she an exchange student?
4. Are Carlos and Gabriel from Argentina?
5. Is Gabriel on vacation?

6. Are Carlos and Gabriel in love with New York City?
7. Are you from Japan?
8. Are you in New York now?

C. Present Tense of *Be*: Questions with *How, Where, Who,* and *What*

	Questions	**Possible Answers**
How		
Greetings	**How are** you?	Fine, thank you.
Age	**How old** is he?	Twenty-five.
Where		
Hometown, Country	**Where** are you from?	I am from Turkey.
Location	**Where** are you?	I'm in New York.
Who		
Identity	**Who** is your roommate?	Mariko.
What		
Information	**What** is your native language?	It's Korean.

4 Write a question for each answer. Use *How, Where, Who,* and *What* in your questions. Then work with a partner. Take turns asking and answering the questions.

1. How are you? _____?

   I'm fine, thanks, but I'm a little homesick.

2. _____?

   I'm from France.

3. _____?

   I'm twenty-five.

4. _____?

   Chantal.

5. _____?

   It's French.

6. _____?

   She's at the hotel right now.

D. Present Tense of *Be*: Negative Statements

Long form	Contraction
I **am not** late.	I**'m not** late.
She / He / It **is not** late.	She**'s** / He**'s** / It**'s not** late.
	She / He / It **isn't** late.
You / We / They **are not** late.	You**'re** / We**'re** / They**'re not** late.
	You / We / They **aren't** late.

5   Use *am*, *is*, or *are* to complete these sentences. Use a contraction form when possible. Use negative forms when you see (not).

1. We <u>'re</u> from Marlboro, Vermont, and we _____ very happy here.
      1   2

   Marlboro _____ (not) very big, so it _____ (not) noisy or crowded. Our
              3   4

   streets _____ (not) dangerous or dirty. Our neighbors _____ friendly, and
             5   6

   our little town _____ very nice.
                     7

E. Using *It* with Weather and Time Expressions

Questions	Possible Answers
What's the weather today?	**It's** beautiful.
What's the weather **like**?	**It's** terrible.
What's it **like** out(side)?	**It's** nice.
What time is **it**?	**It's** eight o'clock.
What day / month / year is **it**?	**It's** Friday / August / 2002.
What's the date (today)?	**It's** August 20th.

6   Work with a partner. Make complete sentences about the weather in these cities.

Example: New York / cloudy and cool
                New York is cloudy and cool today.

1. Madison, Wisconsin / sunny, breezy, and warm

2. Denver, Colorado / cloudy, rainy, and cool

3. Montreal, Quebec / cold and cloudy

4. Tucson, Arizona / very hot and dry

5. San Francisco, California / foggy and cool

6. Toronto, Ontario / very cold and windy

7 Work with a partner. Tell the time, day, or date.

Example: It's 8:15.

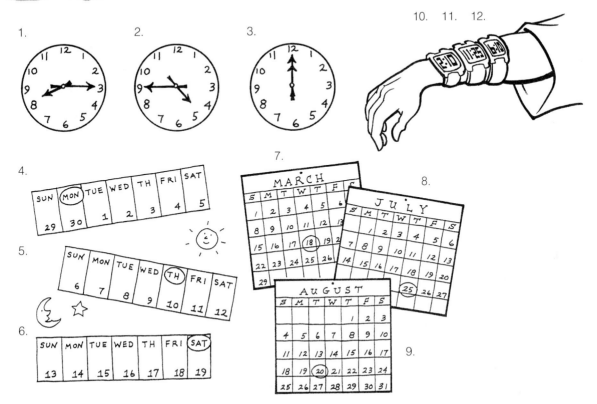

F. Prepositions of Time—*In, On, At, From...To (Until)*

	Period of Time	**Examples**
in	general time of day month season year	Alex was born **in** the afternoon. Alex was born **in** July. Alex was born **in** the summer. Alex was born **in** 1986.
on	days dates also: *weekdays / weekends*	My birthday is **on** Saturday. My birthday is **on** September 20th I work **on** weekdays / weekends.
at	specific times also: *at night*	My class is **at** 8:30 P.M. The party is **at** night.
from...to (until)	beginning and ending times	The party is **from** 8:30 **until** midnight.

8 Circle the correct prepositions.

I'm usually awake (at / on) 6:15 A.M. (in / on) weekdays. I'm at work (from / at)
                   1   2   3
8:00 (in / on) the morning. I work (at / from) 8:00 (in / to) 4:30 (at / in) the
       4   5   6   7
afternoon. Then I'm at school (in / from) 7:00 (on / to) 8:30 (at / in) night.
                                 8   9   10
(In / On) the weekends, I'm very lazy. I'm still in bed (at / from) 10:00 A.M.
 11   12

9 Use *at, in, on, from,* or *to* to complete this reading.

My life in New York City is very busy. My home is far from my work, so __from__
                                                                          1
Monday _____ Friday, I am awake _____ 5:00 _____ the morning. _____ Monday,
        2   3   4   5
Wednesday, and Friday, I take the bus to work. _____ Tuesday and Thursday, I drive
                                                 6
my car. My day is very long. I am usually home _____ 7:30 or 8:00 P.M. _____ the
                                                 7   8
weekend, I sleep late.

G. *There is / There are*—Affirmative and Negative Statements

Affirmative Statements

	Long Form	**Contraction**
With a singular noun	**There is** a museum downtown.	**There's** a museum downtown.
With plural nouns	**There are** many banks downtown.	**There're** many banks downtown.

Note: The contraction *there're* is often used in speech, but it is not usually used in writing.

Negative Statements

	Long Form	**Contraction**
With a singular noun	**There is not** a post office nearby.	**There isn't** a post office nearby.
With plural nouns	**There are not** many stores downtown.	**There aren't** many stores downtown.

10 Use *is* or *are* to complete these sentences.

1. There ____is____ a subway in San Francisco.
2. There _____ many parks in San Francisco.
3. There _____ many hills in San Francisco.
4. There _____ many cable cars.
5. There _____ a wharf for boats called Fisherman's Wharf.
6. There _____ a large Chinese neighborhood in San Francisco.
7. There _____ a tower in San Francisco.
8. There _____ many bridges.

11 Use *isn't* or *aren't* to complete these sentences.

1. There __isn't__ a wharf in Houston.
2. There _____ many large parks.
3. There _____ many rivers.
4. There _____ mountains nearby.
5. There _____ many hills in Houston.
6. There _____ cable cars.
7. There _____ a subway.
8. There _____ snow in Houston.

H. *There is / There are*—Questions and Short Answers

	Questions	Possible Answers	
		Affirmative	Negative
Singular	**Is there** a post office nearby?	Yes, **there is**.	No, **there isn't**.
Plural	**Are there** many stores downtown?	Yes, **there are**.	No, **there aren't**.

12   Ask and answer questions. Use the cues to make questions. Use the map to help you.

Examples:

many bridges to Manhattan

A: Are there many bridges to Manhattan?
B: Yes, there are.

an island in the East River

A: Is there an island in the East River?
B: Yes, there is.

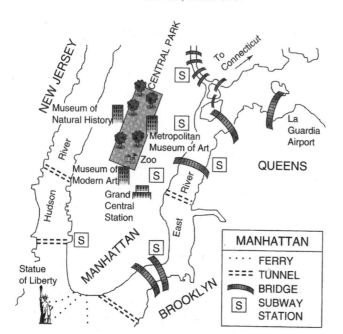

1.   a subway in Manhattan

2.   many tunnels

3.   four rivers around Manhattan

4.   a bridge to the Statue of Liberty

5.   many ferries to Manhattan

6.   a train station in Manhattan

7.   a large park

8.   a zoo in Central Park

9.   many museums in Manhattan

10.   an airport in Manhattan

11.   an airport in Brooklyn

12.   an airport in Queens

I. Prepositions of Place—*In, On, At*

Prepositions	Uses	Examples
in	buildings cities / states / regions / countries	She lives **in** an apartment. Her apartment is **in** Boston. Boston is **in** Massachusetts.
on	bodies of water and coasts streets	Boston is **on** the Charles River, **on** the East Coast. Her apartment is **on** Beacon Street.
at	specific addresses and many specific locations	She lives **at** 121 Beacon Street. She works **at** the bank.

13 Complete these sentences with *at* or *on*.

1. The library is __on__ Second Avenue.
2. The library is _____ 413 Second Avenue.
3. Mariko is _____ the library now.
4. The post office is _____ the river.
5. It's _____ 2020 River Street.
6. Carlos is _____ the post office now.
7. Carlos' apartment is also _____ River Street.
8. My favorite coffee shop is _____ Main Street.

14 Form sentences with *in* or *on*.

Example: Miami / the U.S.A.
Miami is in the U.S.A.

1. Paris / France
2. Geneva / Switzerland
3. Tokyo / Japan
4. Chicago / Lake Michigan
5. San Francisco / the Pacific Ocean
6. Buenos Aires / Argentina
7. Miami / the Atlantic Ocean
8. Cairo / the Nile River

15 Are these sentences true or false? Use negatives to correct the false sentences. Then tell the true location of each place.

Examples:
San Diego and San Francisco are in Oregon.
San Diego and San Francisco aren't in Oregon. They're in California.

1. Santa Barbara is in Oregon.
2. The Cascade Mountains are in Arizona.
3. Reno is on the Pacific Ocean.
4. Vancouver and Edmonton are in Washington.
5. Los Angeles is on the Pacific Ocean.
6. Seattle is on the Columbia River.
7. Phoenix and Tucson are in Nevada.
8. The Grand Canyon is in Arizona.

Video Activities: Venice

Before You Watch.

1. Where is the city of Venice? Circle the correct answer.
    a.   France   b.   Italy   c.   Greece
2. Venice is famous because it has _____.
    a.   old buildings   b.   many canals   c.   a lot of rain

Watch.   Check all the correct answers.

> **Vocabulary Note:** To sink means to go under the water. The past tense is sank.

1. What are Venice's problems?
    _____   The canals are crowded.
    _____   The water is very dirty.
    _____   There is a lot of air pollution
    _____   No one wants to go there.
    _____   It is sinking.
2. Venice needs _____.
    _____   money
    _____   tourists
    _____   water

Watch Again.

1. Complete the sentences with numbers from the box.

200	30	6,000,000	1

    1. Venice has about _____ canals.
    2. A few years ago Venice sank about _____ foot.
    3. They cleaned the canals _____ years ago.
    4. About _____ tourists visit Venice each year.

2. Bob Guthrie's group is called "_____ Venice."
    a.   Visit   b.   Stop   c.   Save

After You Watch.   Each sentence in this paragraph has a grammatical error. Find the errors and rewrite the paragraph correctly.

Venice is Italy. It very old city. Has many canals. Venice have many problems, too. There a lot of air pollution and water pollution. There are a lot of tourist in Venice too. The government of Italy has not money for Venice's problems

Chapter 2

Shopping and e-Commerce

PART 1   Listening to Conversations

Before You Listen

1   **Preparing to Listen.**   Look at these photos.

Photo 1

Photo 2

1.   Describe Photo 1. What kind of shopping is this?
2.   Describe Photo 2. What kind of shopping is this?
3.   What are the differences between these two kinds of shopping?

2   **Vocabulary Preview.**   Ali and Beth go to Alicia's apartment. Alicia is also a student at Faber College.

1.   Listen to these words from their conversation. Circle the ones you don't know.

Nouns
credit card
mall
online shopping
window-shopping

Adjectives
crowded
old-fashioned

Verbs
to do / go shopping
to look for (parking)
to save money / time / energy
to spend money / time / energy

2. Guess the meanings of the underlined words. Write your guess on the lines. Check your answers with a dictionary or your teacher.

   1. I want <u>to go shopping</u> because I need to buy some new clothes.

      My guess: _____

   2. Too many people shop at this place—this store is too <u>crowded</u>!

      My guess: _____

   3. I don't have very much time to go to stores, so I use my computer to do <u>online shopping</u>.

      My guess: _____

   4. Beth doesn't like to carry money so she always uses a <u>credit card</u> to buy things.

      My guess: _____

   5. We're going <u>window-shopping</u>—we're just going to look; we're not going inside the stores.

      My guess: _____

   6. Alicia can <u>save energy</u> if she doesn't drive her car.

      My guess: _____

   7. I like to shop at the <u>mall</u> because there are many different stores there.

      My guess: _____

   8. Beth is <u>old-fashioned</u>—she likes things that are traditional.

      My guess: _____

   9. Ali can't leave his car on the street so he's going <u>to look for parking</u> near the store.

      My guess: _____

   10. I can't go shopping because I can't <u>spend</u> any money.

       My guess: _____

Listen

3 **Listening for Main Ideas.**   Listen to the conversation. As you listen, answer these questions.

1. Where are Beth and Ali going?
2. What kind of shopping does Alicia usually do?
3. Is Alicia going with Beth and Lee?

4 **Listening for Specific Information.**   Listen again. Circle the letter of the best answer to each question.

1. Why does Alicia like online shopping?
   a. She saves money.
   b. She saves time.
   c. She can touch things.

2. What does Ali say about online shopping?
   a. It saves energy.
   b. You don't have to look for parking.
   c. Both a. and b.

3. What does Beth like about shopping at the mall?
   a. You can save money.
   b. You save time.
   c. You can see and touch things.

After You Listen

5 **Understanding Main Ideas.**   Match the statement with a kind of shopping.

a. online shopping   b. window-shopping   c. shopping at the mall

___a___ You save energy.   _____ You can save money.

_____ You can touch things.   _____ You can enjoy a nice day.

_____ You can see things.   _____ It's crowded.

_____ You can save time.   _____ You sit in front of your computer.

_____ You don't have to look   _____ You don't need a credit card.
for parking.

6 **Vocabulary Review.**   Complete these sentences. Use words from the list.

credit card	shopping	mall	look for
spend	online shopping	save	crowded

1. VISA is a _____.
2. When I need some clothes, I go _____ at a store.
3. I don't like stores, so I do _____ instead.
4. I don't have any money, so I'm just going _____ today.
5. We want to shop for three different things, so let's go to the _____.
6. Ali needs to _____ parking before he can go into the mall.
7. I don't have a lot of money, so I don't want to _____ it.
8. Alicia likes to _____ energy, so she isn't driving her car.

Stress

7   **Listening for Stressed Words.**   Listen to the first part of the conversation again.

1.   The stressed words are missing. Fill in the blanks with words from the list.

Ali	good	know	nice
doing	how're	meet	online
Egypt	in	mostly	shopping

Alicia: Hi, Beth. Come on _____in_____ …

                                    1

Beth: Hi, Alicia! _____ you _____?

                            2   3

Alicia: Pretty _____.

                          4

Beth: Alicia, this is my friend _____. He's from _____.

                                                    5   6

Alicia: Hi, Ali. _____ to _____ you.

                            7   8

Ali: Nice to meet you too.

Beth: So, Alicia, we're going to go _____. Do you want to come?

                                                        9

Alicia: Gee, I don't _____ … I _____ do _____

                                  10   11   12

      shopping these days.

2.   Now read the conversation with a partner. Practice stressing words correctly.

Reductions

In normal speech, English speakers do not say some words clearly—they use a reduced form, or reduction. Reductions are like contractions (Chapter 1) except that people do not usually use them in writing.

Example:

Long Form	**Reduced Form**
I don't know.	I dunno.

8 **Comparing Long and Reduced Forms.**   Listen to the following sentences from the conversation. They contain reduced forms. Repeat them after the speaker.

Long Form	Reduced Form
1. <u>How are</u> you <u>doing</u>?	<u>How're</u> you <u>doin'</u>?
2. It's nice to <u>meet you</u>.	It's nice to <u>meetcha</u>.
3. We aren't <u>going to</u> spend any money.	We aren't <u>gonna</u> spend any money.
4. Do you <u>want to</u> come?	Do you <u>wanna</u> come?
5. You don't <u>have to</u> look for parking.	You don't <u>hafta</u> look for parking.

9 **Listening for Reductions.**   Listen and circle the letter of the sentence that you hear. If you hear a reduction*, circle the letter of the reduced sentence, even though it is not a correct written form.

1. a. It's nice to meet you.   b. It's nice to meetcha*.
2. a. Aren't you coming?   b. Arencha* comin'?
3. a. I'm spending too much money.   b. I'm spendin'* too much money.
4. a. Do you want to go shopping?   b. Do you wanna* go shopping?
5. a. Do you have to study today?   b. Do you hafta* study today?

Talk It Over

1. Work in groups of four. Write the names of your group members in the spaces at the top of the chart.

2. Look at the example (Stacy). Practice asking your teacher the questions and write his / her answers on the chart.

    Example:
    What are you doing this weekend?
    I'm going to visit my cousin.

3. Then ask your group members the questions. Write their answers on the chart.

Question	_Stacy_	Teacher	Name	Name	Name
1. What are you doing this weekend?	_Visiting my cousin._				
2. Do you like shopping at the mall? Why? Why not?	_Yes. It's fun._				
3. Do you do online shopping? Why? Why not?	_No. Don't have a computer._				
4. Do you try to save money?	_No._				
5. Do you try to save energy?	_Yes._				
6. Do you try to save time?	_Yes._				
7. Your question:					

PART 2 # Listening Skills

Getting Meaning from Context

1   **Using Context Clues.**

Ali, Alicia, and Beth are window-shopping at a large shopping mall.

1. Listen to their conversation. It is in five parts. Listen to the beginning of each part.

2. Listen to the question. Write the number of the part next to the best answer.

3. Then listen to the last part of the conversation to hear the correct answer.

_____ a clothing store   _____ an ATM (automated teller machine)

_____ a supermarket   _____ a post office

_____ a café   _____ a bookstore

_____ a bakery   _____ a sporting goods store

Listening for Prices

Before You Listen

2 **Preparing to Listen.**   Before you listen, discuss these questions with a partner.

1. Do you ever wear blue jeans? When?
2. What kind (brand) of jeans do you like?
3. Where do you buy jeans?
4. How much are they?

3 **Vocabulary Preview.**   Listen. Circle the words and expressions you don't know.

Noun	**Adjective**	**Expressions**
brand	favorite	the best deal
		the lowest / best / highest price
		on sale
		a pair of (jeans)

Listen

4 **Listening for the Main Idea.**   You are going to listen to three ads for blue jeans. As you listen, answer this question.

What kind of jeans are they? Check (✔) the correct answer.

_____ Western Wonders

_____ Wild West

_____ Wild and Wooly

5 **Listening for Store Names.** Listen again. Draw a line to match the ad number to the store name.

Ad 1

Ad 2

Ad 3

6 **Listening for Prices.** Listen to the ads again. Draw a line to match the price to the store.

$31.99

$35.99

$29.99

7 **Listening to Compare Prices.** Listen to the ads again. Then answer these questions with a partner:

1. Which store has the highest price for Wild West jeans?
2. Where is the best place to buy Wild West jeans? Why?

After You Listen

8 **Comparing Prices and Stores.** In small groups, about the answers to these questions.

1. Where do you usually buy clothes?
2. Which store in your city or town has the best prices for clothes?

Listening to Online Shopping Information

SuperMall.com

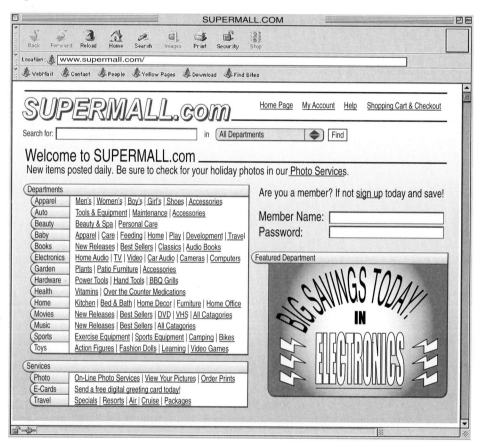

Before You Listen

9 **Preparing to Listen.** Before you listen, talk about the Internet with a partner.

1. What kind of Websites do you like?
2. What kind do you visit or use often?

10 **Vocabulary Preview.** Listen. Circle the words and phrases you don't know.

Nouns		**Verbs**
furniture	purchase	deliver
gift	shipping	fill out (a form)
groceries*	shopping (Web)site	place an order
online shopper	transaction	promise

*This noun is always plural.

Listen

11 **Listening for the Main Idea.** Now listen to the information. As you listen, try to answer this question.

What kind of Website is SuperMall.com?

12 **Listening to Online Shopping Information.** Listen again. This time, listen for the answers to these questions.

1. What two ways is SuperMall.com different from other shopping Websites?

   First way: _____

   Second way: _____

2. What kinds of things can you buy at SuperMall.com? List three:

   _____

   _____

3. You order something from SuperMall.com at 1 P.M. on Tuesday. You receive it at (circle the correct time):
   a. 5 P.M. on Tuesday   b. 2 P.M. on Wednesday   c. 2 P.M. on Tuesday

4. How does SuperMall.com save time?

   _____

   _____

After You Listen

13 **Discussing Online Shopping.** In small groups, answer these questions.

1. What are some advantages to (good things about) online shopping? What are some disadvantages (bad things)?
2. Do you use shopping Websites? Why or why not?
3. Will shopping online be different in the future? How?

| PART 3 | # Reading |

Before You Read

1 Discuss the following questions with a partner or in small groups.

1. Do you have a computer? Do any of your friends have computers?
2. Do you use the Internet? Do any of your friends use the Internet?
3. Did you know about the Internet two years ago? Five years ago? Ten years ago?
4. Do you shop on the Internet? What do you buy on the Internet?

2 **Vocabulary Preview.**   Sometimes a dictionary isn't necessary to find the meaning of a new word. The meaning is sometimes in parentheses ( ).

Example: Many people are <u>online</u> (using the Internet).

What is *online*? _using the Internet_

Write the meaning of the underlined word on the line.

1. Amazon.com has 10 million <u>customers</u> (people who buy things).
   What are *customers*? _____

2. You can visit <u>virtual</u> (not real) shopping malls online.
   What is *virtual*? _____

3. They sell <u>home improvement products</u> (things you use to fix up a house).
   What is a *home improvement product*? _____

3 **Making Good Guesses.**   Circle the letter to complete the sentence.

1. We bought the house for $100,000. We sold it for $110,000. We made a $10,000 <u>profit</u>.

   A <u>profit</u> is most likely _____.

   a. money you lose in business

   b. money you make in business

   c. money you pay for a house

2. Jeff Bezos had very little money. The company began in a <u>garage</u>, and at first there were very few customers.

   A <u>garage</u> is most likely a _____.

   a. big, expensive house

   b. place to play baseball

   c. small, inexpensive building

4 **Using Verbs.** We can use *(be) going to* to talk about the future. *Going to* is pronounced "gonna" in speech.

Write a sentence with *going to*. Share it with a partner.

subject	future form	verb phrase
The Internet	is going to	continue to grow.
People	are going to	shop online.

Many common verbs are irregular in the past tense. Do you know the verbs in the box? Work with a partner. Use some of the verbs in sentences. Use both tenses.

Present Tense	Past Tense
know	knew
is	was
have	had
quit	quit
drive	drove
begin	began
sell	sold
think	thought

Read

5 Read the article. Don't use your dictionary. If you don't know some words, try to figure out their meaning.

Internet Shopping

A Twenty years ago very few people used the Internet. Only scientists and people in the government knew about the Internet and how to use it. This is changing very fast. Now almost everyone knows about the Internet, and many people are online (using the Internet) every day. When people think about the Internet, they often think about information. But now, more and more, when people think about the Internet, they think about shopping.

B Amazon.com was one of the first companies to try to sell products on the Internet. Jeff Bezos started the company. He was a successful vice-president of a company in New York. One day he had a vision of the future. He thought, "The World Wide Web is growing 2000% a year. It's going to continue to grow. Shopping is going to move to the Internet. People are going to shop online." He quit his good job and drove across the country to Seattle, Washington. There he started an online bookstore called Amazon.com. Bezos had very

little money. The company began in a garage, and at first there were very few customers (people who buy things).

C   At the Amazon.com site, people can search for a book about a subject, find many different books about that subject, read what other people think about the books, order them by credit card, and get them in the mail in two days. This kind of bookstore was a new idea, but the business grew. In a few years, Amazon.com had 10 million customers and listed (sold) 18 million different items in categories including books, CDs, toys, electronics, videos, DVDs, home improvement products (things you use to fix up a house), software, and video games. Today you can buy anything from gourmet food to caskets at a "virtual shopping mall," that is, a group of stores all over the world that functions like a group of stores all in one place.

Jeff Bezos

D   Are people going to shop online more and more? No one knows for sure. Online shopping is growing, but it may not make money for companies like Amazon.com. Jeff Bezos is a billionaire, but his billions of dollars are invested in the company; even after several years, Amazon.com was still not making a profit. If online shopping continues to grow, Bezos hopes his investment will produce real profits.

After You Read

6 **Finding the Main Ideas.**   Circle the letter to complete the sentence.

1. The title of the article is "Internet Shopping." Another possible title is _____.
   a. "Internet Games"
   b. "Shopping on the Internet"
   c. "Information and the Internet"

2. The main idea of Paragraph A is _____.
   a. Nowadays more and more people use the Internet, especially to shop
   b. Twenty years ago very few people used the Internet
   c. Scientists were first to use the Internet

3. The main idea of Paragraph B is _____.
   a. The Web is growing 2000% a year
   b. Amazon.com. is an example of a company that sells on the Internet
   c. Jeff Bezos quit his good job and moved to Seattle, Washington

4. The main idea of Paragraph C is _____.
   a. People can order books by credit card
   b. Amazon.com grew
   c. People can search for a book on Amazon.com

5. The main idea of Paragraph D is _____.
   a. Online shopping is going to grow.
   b. Jeff Bezos is a billionaire.
   c. Online shopping may or may not grow.

Organizing a Reading

"Internet Shopping" is a typical information article. The organization is very simple:

1. Introduction of the subject (paragraph A)
2. A good example (paragraph B)
3. More details of that example (paragraph C)
4. Conclusion (paragraph D)

Synopsis

You can say the main information in "Internet Shopping" in a short paragraph. This is called a *synopsis*. A synopsis gives the main ideas of a reading or an article. Here is a synopsis of "Internet Shopping."

Many people are now shopping on the Internet. One example is the online book-store Amazon.com. Amazon.com has a lot of customers, but it is not making a profit yet. No one knows the future of online shopping.

Understanding Quotation Marks

We use quotation marks to tell what someone says or thinks. For example:

He thought, "The World Wide Web is growing 2000 percent a year."

Discussing the Reading

7 Discuss the following questions. Then share your answers with the class.

1. Do any of your friends spend a lot of time online? Is this good or bad?
2. Some people shop for food on the Internet. Do you think Internet shopping is going to get bigger and more important in the future?

PART 4   # Writing

Using Sentence Patterns

Sentence Pattern 3.   The most common pattern in English sentences is subject + verb + object.

> **subject**   +   **verb**   +   **object**
> The car   hit   the tree.
>
> Note that the **subject** in this sentence is the actor; it (the car) is doing the action. The **verb** is the action the actor performed. The tree is receiving the action. A verb that has both an actor and a receiver of the action is called a *transitive* verb.

Sentence Pattern 4.   Some verbs don't take an object. They are complete with only a subject and a verb.

> **subject**   +   **verb**
> The man   jumped.
>
> The action of the verb doesn't cause something to happen to someone or something else. Instead there's only an actor and the action. This kind of verb is called an *intransitive* verb.
>
> With intransitive verbs, there is often a prepositional phrase after the verb that tells us where, when, or how the action happened.
>
> **subject**   +   **verb**   +   **prepositional phrase**
> The man   jumped   in the pool.
>
> Note that many verbs can be both transitive and intransitive.

Do the following sentences use Sentence Pattern 3 or 4? Write 3 or 4 in the space.

_____3_____ 1. Fifteen or twenty years ago very few people used the Internet.

_____ 2. But his business grew.

_____ 3. Bezos had a vision of the future.

_____ 4. He quit his good job.

_____ 5. He started an online bookstore called Amazon.com.

_____ 6. The company began in a garage.

_____ 7. The World Wide Web is growing.

_____ 8. Some people don't like this idea.

Practicing the Writing Process

Read a student's prediction of a new plant.

> A new plant is going to be very popular. It is called a <u>tomana</u>. It is a combination of a tomato and a banana. The tomana looks like a red banana but it smells like a tomato. The outside peel (skin) is very thick and protects the fruit inside. It is easy to peel the tomana. When you remove the peel, you have a perfect tomato / banana. It is easy to slice the peeled tomana for salads or sandwiches.

1 **Exploring Ideas: Free Writing.** One way to get ideas is to "freewrite." When you freewrite, you write for ten minutes about your idea. Do not worry about your spelling or grammar. Just try to get a lot of ideas down. Your teacher does not correct or look at a freewrite.

The purpose of a freewrite is simply to help you get ideas. Sometimes if you can't think of anything to say, just write "I can't think of anything to say" many times. The main thing is to keep on writing. For example, you can write about a new combination of two fruits or vegetables, like the *tomana* in the student's prediction. What does the new fruit / vegetable look like? What does it smell like? What does it taste like? Or write about a new machine of the future that does some difficult job. What does it do? What does it look like?

Now tell a partner or a group about your prediction. Don't read your freewrite aloud but use the ideas from it.

When we want to describe someone or something, we often make a comparison between the two persons or things. To do so, we often use a verb of perception (smell, feel, look, sound, taste) with the word *like*.

Example:

My brother looks *like* my sister.

Think about your prediction. Can you complete this sentence about it?

It looks like _____

_____ .

What does it smell like? What does it sound, feel, or taste like?

2   **Writing the First Draft.**   Now write the first draft of your prediction.

3   **Editing.**   After writing your first draft, it's time to edit your work. Here is a checklist of things to look for in your paragraph.

Editing Checklist

1. Do your sentences begin with capital letters?

2. Do other words in your paragraph need capital letters?

3. Do your sentences end with periods or other final punctuation?

4. Do any words in your paragraph need a comma after them?

5. Are the words spelled correctly? (Use your dictionary!)

6. Do you have interesting details?

4   **Peer Editing.**   Show your paragraph to a partner. Read each other's paragraphs. Are there interesting details? Is the description clear?

5   **Writing the Second Draft.**   Now write the second draft of your prediction. Then give it to your teacher.

Writing a Journal

6   Write a journal entry about your plans for the future. Use *going to* and past tense verbs if you can.

I'm going to study chemistry. I want to be a chemist.
My sister is going to study medicine. She wants to be a doctor.

PART 5	# Grammar

A. Present Continuous Tense: Affirmative Statements

Long Form	Contraction	Notes
I **am looking**. You **are looking**. He / she / it **is looking**. We / you / they **are looking**.	I**'m looking**. You**'re looking**. He**'s** / she**'s** / it**'s looking**. We**'re** / you**'re** / they**'re looking**.	The present continuous tense tells about actions in progress now. Some time expressions with this tense are *now* and *right now*.

Note: Sometimes the spelling of the verb changes when you add *-ing*.

Verbs ending in a consonant and *e*: Drop *e* and add *-ing*: drive—driving.

Verbs ending in one vowel and one consonant: Double the consonant and add *-ing*: shop—shopping.

1 Use the present continuous to complete these sentences. Use the picture below and the verbs in parentheses for help.

1. Mike __is buying__ (buy) gifts.
2. The little boys _____ (run).
3. The little girl and her mother _____ (take) a walk.
4. They _____ (look) at toys.
5. The teenage girls _____ (shop) for new clothes.
6. The woman _____ (go) home.
7. The teenage boy _____ (listen) to music.
8. The old man _____ (read) the newspaper.
9. Many people _____ (shop).

B. Present Continuous Tense: Negative Statements

Long Form	Contraction	
I **am not working**. He / she / it **is not working**. You / we / they **are not working**.	I**'m not working**. He**'s** / she**'s** / it**'s not working**. You**'re** / we**'re** / they**'re not working**.	He / she / it **isn't working**. You / we / they **aren't working**.

2 These sentences have negative contractions. Give the other form of each negative contraction.

Example:
> We're not spending money.
> *We aren't spending money.*

1. She's not buying new clothes.
2. He isn't using a credit card.
3. They're not spending money.
4. We're not eating in restaurants.
5. It's not working.
6. You're not driving the car often.
7. We're not shopping online.
8. They aren't looking at catalogues.

C. Present Continuous Tense: Yes / No Questions and Short Answers

	Affirmative	Negative
Are you **looking**? **Is** he / she / it **looking**?	Yes, **I am**. Yes, **he / she / it is**.	No, **I'm not**. No, **he / she / it isn't**. No, **he's / she's / it's not**.
Are we / you / they **looking**?	Yes, **we / you / they are**.	No, **we / you / they aren't**. No, **we're / you're / they're not**.

3 Work with a partner. Take turns asking and answering these questions about the picture in Activity 1.

Example:
> A: Is the woman carrying packages?
> B: Yes, she is.

1. Is the old man reading a book?
2. Are the little boys running?
3. Are the boys riding bicycles?
4. Is the teenage boy dancing?
5. Is the little girl walking with her father?
6. Are we studying math now?
7. Are you studying English now?
8. Are you speaking Chinese now?

D. More Prepositions of Place

to the left / right of	next to	across from
over / under	between	in front of / in back of
near / far from	on top of	

4   Look at this map of the mall. Complete these sentences with *next to*, *across from*, etc.

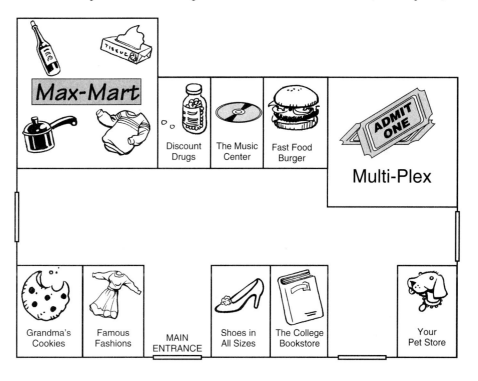

1. There is a drugstore _____ Max-Mart.

2. There is a music store _____ Discount Drugs and Fast Food Burger.

3. There is a cinema _____ Grandma's Cookies.

4. There is a drug store _____ the music store.

5. There is a bookstore_____ a fast food restaurant.

6. There is an entrance _____ the College Bookstore.

7. There is a pet store _____ the College Bookstore.

Video Activities: Online Pharmacies

Before You Watch.

1. Which of these stores sell medicine?
    a. a pharmacy   b. a bakery   c. a hardware store
2. What is a prescription?
    a. a kind of medicine
    b. doctor's permission to buy a type of medicine

Watch.

1. What is the message of this video?
    a. Don't buy drugs online.
    b. Be careful when you buy drugs online.
    c. Always buy drugs online.

2. What is happening to drug sales on the Internet?
    a. More and more people are buying drugs online.
    b. Not many people are buying drugs online.
    c. Online pharmacies are not popular.

Watch Again.

1. Complete the following chart.

    Sale of Drugs Online

Year	Amount
2000	_____
2001	$ 400, 000, 000
____	$1,100,000,000
2003	_____
____	_____

2. Check the benefits of buying drugs online
    _____ accountability   _____ convenience
    _____ price   _____ privacy
    _____ reliability   _____ safety

After You Watch.

Combine the following sentences with *and . . . too* or *but*.

1. I'm buying books on line. My friend is buying books on line too.
2. Many people are buying lifestyle drugs online. They aren't buying antibiotics.
3. An antibiotic kills germs. A lifestyle drug doesn't kill germs.
4. You need a prescription to buy antibiotics. You need a prescription to buy lifestyle drugs.
5. Online bookstores are popular. Online pharmacies are popular.

Chapter 3

Friends and Family

PART 1

Listening to Conversations

Before You Listen

1 **Preparing to Listen.** Look at these photos.

Photo 1

Photo 2

1. Describe the photos. What are the people doing? Who are they?
2. How often do you talk to your family? How often do you talk to your friends?

2 **Vocabulary Preview.** Ali and Beth are going to a movie. They ask Lee to come.

1. Listen to these words from their conversation. Circle the ones you don't know.

Noun	Verbs	Expression
phone card	to be / get homesick (for)	by letter / phone / e-mail
	to guess	
	to miss	
	to stay / keep in touch	

2. Guess the meanings of the underlined words. Write your guess on the lines. Check your answers with a dictionary or your teacher.

    1. I see that your clothes are wet. I <u>guess</u> it's raining.

        My guess: _____

    2. Lee doesn't see his family often and he feels sad. I think that he's <u>homesick</u>.

        My guess: _____

    3. After you move, please <u>keep in touch</u> with me so I know how you're doing.

        My guess: _____

4. Ali only calls his father once a month because it's expensive to keep in touch <u>by phone</u>.

    My guess: _____

5. Alicia uses her computer all day, so she keeps in touch with friends <u>by e-mail</u>.

    My guess: _____

6. To save money, Lee keeps in touch with his parents <u>by letter</u>.

    My guess: _____

7. I haven't seen you in a long time and I feel sad about that. I <u>miss</u> you very much!

    My guess: _____

8. I don't like to carry a lot of change, so I use a <u>phone card</u> and call from pay phones.

    My guess: _____

Listen

3 **Listening for the Main Idea.**   Listen to the conversation. As you listen, answer this question.
   Why is Lee homesick?

4 **Listening for Specific Information.**   Listen again. Circle the letter of the best answer to each question.

1. How often does Lee get letters from his family?
    a. One or two times a month.
    b. Two or three times a week.
    c. Two or three times a month.
2. How does Beth stay in touch with her friends and family?
    a. She stays in touch by phone.
    b. She stays in touch by e-mail.
    c. She stays in touch by letter.
3. How does Ali keep in touch with his friends and family?
    a. He stays in touch by phone.
    b. He stays in touch by e-mail.
    c. He stays in touch by letter.
4. What does Ali say about e-mail?
    a. It's inexpensive.
    b. It's expensive.
    c. It's difficult.
5. What do Beth and Ali do to help Lee?
    a. They tell him to write a letter to his parents.
    b. They tell him to call his parents.
    c. They tell him to buy a phone card.

After You Listen

5   **Discussing Main Ideas.**   Work with a partner. Discuss the answers to these questions.

1. How does Lee feel at first?
2. How do you think he feels after Ali and Beth talk to him?
   When you are away from home, do you ever feel homesick? If yes, what do you do to feel better?

6   **Vocabulary Review.**   Complete these sentences. Use words from the list.

to keep in touch	by e-mail	to guess
to be homesick	to miss	by letter

1. Lee likes _____ with his family in Korea to hear all their news.
2. I'm going _____ my family when I leave them.
3. Since he is far away from them, it's natural for Lee _____ for his family in Korea.
4. I don't know the answer. I'm going _____.
5. I don't have a computer, so I can't keep in touch _____.
6. I like to write in English, so I'm going to keep in touch with you _____.

Stress

7   **Listening for Stressed Words.**   Listen to the first part of the conversation again.

1. The stressed words are missing. Fill in the blanks with words from the list.

Beth	I	minute	OK	What
family	Lee	miss	reading	why
homesick	letter	movie	sad	with

Ali: Hi, _____! _____ and _____ are
         going to see a _____. Come _____ us.

Lee: _____. Just a _____.

Beth: _____ are you _____, Lee?

Lee: A _____ from my _____.

Beth: But _____ are you so _____?

Lee: I _____ them. I guess I'm _____.

2.   Now read the conversation with a partner. Practice stressing words correctly.

Reductions

8   **Comparing Long and Reduced Forms.**   Listen to the following sentences from the conversation. They contain reduced forms. Repeat them after the speaker.

Long Form	**Reduced Form**
1. Beth <u>and</u> I are <u>going to</u> see a movie.	Beth <u>'n</u> I are <u>gonna</u> see a movie.
2. <u>What are</u> you reading, Lee?	<u>What're</u> you reading, Lee?
3. <u>Why are</u> you so sad?	<u>Why're</u> you so sad?
4. I miss <u>them</u>.	I miss <u>'em</u>.
5. You <u>can</u> use my phone card.	You <u>c'n</u> use my phone card.

9   **Listening for Reductions.**   Listen and circle the letter of the sentence that you hear. If you hear a reduction*, circle the letter of the reduced sentence, even though it is not a correct written form.

1.   a.   Are you going to come with us?   b.   Are you gonna* come with us?
2.   a.   I don't miss them very much.   b.   I don't miss 'em* very much.
3.   a.   I can go to the movies with you.   b.   I c'n* go to the movies with you.
4.   a.   What are you doing?   b.   What're you doing?
5.   a.   Beth and I are studying.   b.   Beth 'n* I are studying.
6.   a.   Why are you sad?   b.   Why're you sad?

Talk It Over

Do you have any friends or family that live far away? How do you keep in touch with them?

1.   Work in groups of four. Write the names of your group members in the spaces at the top of the chart.
2.   Look at the example (Stacy). Practice asking your teacher the questions and write his / her answers on the chart.

Example: A: Do you have friends who live far away?
B: Yes.
A: Who?
B: My friend Susie.
A: Do you keep in touch?
B: Yes.

3.   Then ask your group members the questions and write their answers on the chart.

Questions	_Stacy_	Teacher	Name	Name	Name
1. Do you have friends or family who live far away?	_Yes._				
2. Who?	_My friend Susie._				
3. Do you keep in touch?	_Yes._				
4. Do you talk to _____ on the phone?	_No, it's too expensive_				
5. Do you e-mail _____?	_Almost every day._				
6. Do you write letters to _____?	_No, never._				

PART 2

Listening Skills

Getting Meaning from Context

1   **Using Context Clues.**

1. Listen to the first part of each conversation.
2. Listen to the question and circle the letter of the best answer.
3. Then listen to the last part to hear the correct answer.

1. What is Lee homesick for?
   - a. his family
   - b. Seoul
   - c. Sue

2. Who does Lee want to call him?
   - a. Sue
   - b. Ali
   - c. no one

3. How many children are in Alicia's family?
   - a. one
   - b. two
   - c. three

4. What's Ali doing?
   - a. writing a letter
   - b. talking on the phone
   - c. reading a letter

5. When can Beth get the cheapest rates?
   - a. this weekend
   - b. in five to ten minutes
   - c. after 5 o'clock today

Listening to Voicemail Messages

Before You Listen

2 **Preparing to Listen.** Before you listen, talk about voicemail with a partner.

1. Why do people have voicemail or answering machines?
2. How do you feel if you miss a phone call?
3. Do you like to leave voicemail messages? Why or why not?

3 **Vocabulary Preview.** Listen. Circle the verbs you don't know.

Verbs

to call someone back	to leave a message
to come by	to look forward to something
to expect someone	to miss a call

Listen

4 **Listening for the Main Idea.** Listen to David's voicemail messages. As you listen, answer this question.

How many people left messages for David?

5 **Listening to Voicemail.** Listen again. This time, write the number of each message below the picture that matches it.

_____ _____

_____ _____ _____

After You Listen

6 **Discussing Voicemail.**   In small groups, talk about the answers to these questions.

1. Do you have voicemail? Do you have an answering machine? Why or why not?
2. Do most of your friends have voicemail or an answering machine? Why or why not?
3. Describe the best kind of outgoing message (the message that callers hear). Should you give your name? Why or why not? Should you say that you are "not in"? Why or why not?

Listening to Descriptions of People

Before You Listen

7 **Preparing to Listen.** Look at the picture of Ali. Describe him to a partner.

8 **Vocabulary Preview.**   Listen. Circle the words and phrases you don't know.

Adjectives	**Verbs**
slender	to recognize
tall	to wear glasses

Listen

9 **Listening for the Main Idea.**   Beth is describing her friend Sue. Listen to the conversation. Who is Beth describing? Circle the number of the correct photo.

Photo 1

Photo 2

10 **Listening to Descriptions of People.** Listen again. Answer the questions.

1. What color is Sue's hair?
    a. blond   b. red   c. black
2. Which word describes Sue's height?
    a. tall   b. short   c. medium
3. What else do you know about Sue?
    a. She has green eyes.   b. She wears glasses.   c. She has freckles.

After You Listen

11 **Discussing Appearance.** How would you describe yourself on the phone to someone you have never met? Tell your partner.

| PART 3 | **Reading** |

Before You Read

1 Answer these questions about the photos.

1. How many people are in each photo? Who are they?

Photo 1

Photo 2

Photo 3

2 **Vocabulary Preview.**   Learning words in groups that go together will help you learn vocabulary. For example, *marriage*, *partnership*, and *union* all mean a kind of "joining together." Answer these questions in small groups.

1.   Which word from the group *marriage, partnership, union* would you apply to these situations?

    a.   countries that decide to use the same money system

    b.   a man and a woman who make a life together

    c.   workers from one industry

    d.   two women who want to make a life together

    e.   two people who start a new business

    f.   two men who want to make a life together

2.   Which word from the group *family, blended family, extended family* would you apply to these situations?

    a.   a man, a woman, their two children, and a nephew that they are raising

    b.   a man, a woman, their child

    c.   a man with two children who marries a woman with three children

    d.   a woman with one child

    e.   a man, a woman, their two children, and the man's mother who lives with them

    f.   a man and a woman who aren't married but who live together

Read

3 Read the following material quickly. Then do the exercises.

Changing Families

A | Families in almost every country are changing. In North Africa, in the past, many people lived in extended families. Fifty to a hundred people lived together in a group of houses. These were all family members—grandparents, aunts, uncles, cousins, children, and grandchildren. But now this traditional family is breaking into smaller groups.

B | The traditional Japanese family was also an extended family—a son, his parents, his wife, his children, and his unmarried brothers and sisters. They lived together in his parents' home. But this tradition is changing. Now most adults do not live with their parents. They have new problems. Men and women spend a lot of time at work. They don't spend a lot of time together as a family. This can be very difficult.

C | In Europe, in traditional families, the woman stayed home with the children and the man had a job. But families all over Europe are changing. The number of divorces is going up. The number of single-parent families is going up too. In Sweden, more than 40 percent (40%) of all children have parents that are not married. More and more countries are recognizing gay partnerships and marriages. For example, Denmark, Sweden, Norway, the Netherlands, Hungary, and the U.S. state of Vermont all recognize these as legal unions. In much of Europe, many people live alone. In France, more than

D

26 percent of women between age thirty and thirty-four live alone, and more than 27 percent of men of the same age live alone.

There are also big changes in Quebec, Canada. In 1965, a traditional family was important. Almost 90 percent of men and 93.5 percent of women were married. But in 1985, only 49 percent of men and 51.7 percent of women were married! Now more than one-third (⅓) of all babies have parents that are not married. More than one-third of all marriages end in divorce.

E

There are many new types of families. The world is changing, and families are changing too.

After You Read

4 **Finding the Main Ideas.** Circle a letter for each blank.

1. The main idea is that ____ .
    a. in North Africa, families are big, but in Europe, they're small
    b. families around the world are changing
    c. ⅓ of all marriages end in divorce

2. The writer thinks that new families are ____ .
    a. good because they are small
    b. different from families in the past
    c. bad because people don't live together

5 **Understanding Pronouns.** Find and circle the meaning of each underlined pronoun. Then draw an arrow from the pronoun to its meaning.

1. (Fifty to a hundred people) live together in a group of houses. These are all family members.

2. Men and women spend a lot of time at work. They don't spend a lot of time together as a family.

3. They don't spend a lot of time together as a family. This can be very difficult.

4. More and more countries are recognizing gay partnerships and marriages. For example, Denmark, Sweden, Norway, the Netherlands, Hungary, and the U.S. state of Vermont all recognize these as legal unions.

Discussing the Reading

6 Talk about your answers to these questions with your classmates.

1. What kind of family do you live in?
2. Why are families in some countries smaller than in the past?
3. Why are there more single-parent families now?

PART 4

Writing

Using the Simple Present Tense

1 Read this letter to a pen pal. (Pen pals are persons who write to each other but may never have met.) The letter is from a real student from Los Angeles.

Dear Pen Pal,

My name is María González. I am 20 years old. I live in Los Angeles, California. I live with my friends from Mexico. I work in a clothing factory, decorating clothes. For example, I sew jewelry on fancy dresses. Sometimes movie stars wear them.

I like to listen to Mexican banda music. Banda music is like a cross between American country music and rock and roll, but the bands sing in Spanish. I like to read, and I enjoy ice skating. In Los Angeles, you have to go ice skating at indoor skating rinks, because it never gets cold enough outside for ice. It's fun to go ice skating when it's 90 degrees outside.

My favorite TV programs are the National Geographic specials. I like them because I am very interested in foreign countries. I would like to travel to China and France some day.

Sincerely yours,

María González

Write three interesting things about María.

Example:
María is from Mexico.

1. _____

2. _____

3. _____

In Chapter 2 you practiced the simple past tense and the *going to* future tense. The simple present tense is used to talk about things that are true without referring to the past or the future. For example, Maria's sentences in her letter are mostly in the simple present. When you wrote about Maria in the previous activity, you used verbs in the third-person singular form.

Third-Person Singular Endings

We often use the simple present tense when we talk about our everyday lives.

> I go to school four days a week.

Remember, if the subject is third person singular (*he*, *she*, or *it*), we add *-s* or *-es* to the verb.

> My brother works every day.
> He goes to school at night.

Practicing the Writing Process

2 **Exploring Ideas: Using Personal Information.** Write information about yourself in the blanks. Use Maria's letter to help you.

1. My name is _____.

2. I am _____ years old.

3. I live _____.

4. On weekends I like to _____.

5. I like _____. (music, movies, etc.)

6. _____ .

7. _____ .

8. _____ .

Now interview a classmate. First write down the questions to ask. Then fill in the blanks with your classmate's answers.

1. What's your name? _____

   _____ 's name is _____.

2. _____?

   _____ is _____ years old.

3. _____?

   _____.

4. _____ on weekends?

5. _____?

_____ likes _____ .

6. _____ .

7. _____ .

8. _____ .

3 **Writing the First Draft.** Write a pen-pal letter to María. Or perhaps your teacher will help you find a real pen pal in another country. This can be done on the Internet. You can send your letter by e-mail.

4 **Editing.** When you write about something, be very specific and add details (extra or special information). That way your writing will be more interesting.

General (not interesting):

I like music.

Specific (more interesting):

I like classic rock and roll from the sixties, especially the Rolling Stones and the Beatles. I have a hundred CDs.

General (not interesting):

I live in Tokyo.

Specific (more interesting):

I live in Tokyo, the capital city of Japan. There are 12 million people in Tokyo.

Another way to be specific is to include details by adding a second sentence beginning with "For example."

I like to run. For example, last month I ran in a 14-mile marathon.

Rewrite these sentences and make them more interesting and specific. You can use your own information or your imagination.

Example:

~~I like movies.~~

I like science fiction movies. For example, my favorite movie is *Star Wars Episode I: The Phantom Menace.*

1. ~~I like movies.~~

_____

_____

2. ~~I like music:~~

_____

_____

3. ~~I like sports:~~

_____

_____

Now look back at Activity 2. Can you make your answers for Nos. 3, 4, and 5 more interesting? Try to add details, for example.

3. I live _____.

4. On weekends I like to _____.

5. I like _____. (music, movies, etc.)

Next check your pen-pal letter. Use this checklist to correct any mistakes.

Editing Checklist

1. Are sentences in the simple present talking about an action in general?

2. Are the simple present verbs in the simple form (go, watch, play, shop)?

3. Do the third-person singular verb forms end in *-s* or *-es*?

4. Are there good details? (I like rap music, especially Dr. Dre.)

5. Do your sentences begin with capital letters?

6. Do other words in your writing need capital letters?

5   **Peer Editing.**   Show your writing to another student. Can you think of more details? Ask your classmate questions.

6   **Writing the Second Draft.**   Now you are ready to write your second draft. When finished, give it to your teacher.

Writing a Journal

7   Write a journal entry about your everyday activities. Use the simple present tense.

I get up early every day. I take the bus to school. I have classes until two o'clock. Then I go home for a big lunch.

PART 5

Grammar

A. Simple Present Tense: *Have*—Affirmative Statements

Subject + *have*	Subject + *has*
I / you / we / they **have** a problem.	He / she / it **has** a problem.

1   Use *have* or *has* to complete these sentences.

1.   I'm Steve Mason. Loretta and I _have_ a small family. I come from a bigger family.
     I _____ three sisters and two brothers. All of us are married. We all
     _____ children, too. So my mother _____ eleven grandchildren.

2.   I'm Ricky Jones. We _____ a very small family. I _____ only a
     mother. My mother _____ a brother and a sister, and her brother
     _____ two children, so we _____ a lot of relatives.

B. Simple Present Tense: *Do*—Affirmative Statements

Subject + *do*	Subject + *does*
I / you / they / we **do** a lot of work.	She / he / it **does** a lot of work.
do + noun	**do + verb + -ing**
do dishes **do** homework	**do** cleaning **do** (grocery) shopping

2   Use *do* or *does* to complete this reading.

   We have a lot of housework in the Somma family. We all __do__ chores in our
house. My mother _____ the grocery shopping. She also _____ the laundry, but
my older sisters _____ the ironing. My younger sisters _____ the vacuuming.
I _____ the dishes every morning, and my brother _____ the dishes every night.
My father _____ most of the cooking. He also _____ the yard work. We all
_____ housework every day. We try hard to keep our house clean!

C. Simple Present Tense: Other Verbs— Affirmative Statements

Subject + verb	Subject + verb + *s*	Notes
I / you / we / they **work** a lot.	He / she / it **works** a lot.	The simple present tense is used to talk about facts, opinions, and habits or schedules. Time expressions with this tense include *every day, every week, always,* and *sometimes.*

3   Use the verb at the beginning of each paragraph to complete the reading.

work (s)

Joe Somma is nineteen years old. He ___works___ at a grocery store. He _____
                                          1   2
forty hours a week. His younger brother _____ at a car wash. They _____
                                              3   4
part-time, ten hours a week. Joe's father _____ at a gas station, and his mother
                                               5
_____ at a department store. They all _____ very hard!
      6   7

love (s)

Grandpa Somma is eighty years old. He ___loves___ his family. Every afternoon he
                                            8
_____ to visit his grandchildren. They _____ Grandpa Somma. He
      9   10
_____ to tell stories. They _____ the stories.
   11   12

D. Adverbs of Frequency

Adverbs of frequency tell how often something happens.					
100% of the time					0% of the time
always	usually generally	often	sometimes	seldom rarely	never

4   Work with a partner. Tell about your *own* habits and activities. Use one of these adverbs in each sentence: *always, usually, often, sometimes, seldom, rarely, never.*

Example: go to bed late   *I sometimes go to bed late.*

1. get up early
2. eat a big breakfast
3. take the bus to school
4. walk to school

5. have lunch
6. do my homework
7. read the newspaper
8. cook dinner

E. Simple Present Tense: Negative Statements

Long Forms	Contractions
I / you / we / they **do not wash** dishes.	I / you / we / they **don't wash** dishes.
She / he / it **does not wash** dishes.	She / he / it **doesn't wash** dishes.

Note: Don't and *doesn't* are auxiliary or helping verbs. Use them to make present tense verbs negative, except the verb *be.*

5   Use *don't* or *doesn't* to complete these sentences. Then decide if the statements are true. Write *true* or *false* after each statement.

1.   Most people ____don't____ like to do chores. ____true____

2.   My family _____ travel often. _____

3.   We _____ have pets at home. _____

4.   My friends _____ like to go to the movies. _____

5.   Ricky Jones _____ doesn't have brothers or sisters. _____

6.   My best friend _____ study English. _____

7.   I _____ have a lot of time to do chores. _____

8.   Our teacher _____ give us enough homework. _____

F. Simple Present Tense: *Yes / No* Questions

Do + subject + verb	*Does* + subject + verb
Do I / you / we / they **clean** every day?	**Does** he / she / it **help** very often?

6   Ask and answer the following questions. Listen when your partner asks a question. Don't read the question. Look only at each other!

Student A

1.   Do you have a small family or a large family?
2.   Do all of the people in your family live in this city?
3.   Do you often call or e-mail your friends?
4.   Do your relatives speak English?
5.   Now ask two more questions with *do* or *does.*

Student B

1. Does your family take a vacation together?
2. Does your father cook?
3. Do your brothers or sisters speak English?
4. Do your friends call you long-distance?
5. Now ask two more questions with *do* or *does*.

G. The Simple Present Versus the Present Continuous

	Examples	**Notes**
Simple present tense	I always **tell** my friends everything.	The simple present tense is used for facts, opinions, or repeated actions. (See page 65.)
Present continuous tense	Right now he**'s telling** a story to his friend.	The present continuous tense is used for actions that are happening now. (See page 45.)

7   **Information Gap.**   Here are two charts with different information. Ask a partner questions to complete your chart.

Example: B: What is Sally doing now?
           A: What does John do every Monday morning?

		Student A	
	Now	**Every Monday Morning**	**Every Saturday Night**
Sally	sleep		
Sam		work at a restaurant	
John	eat a snack		
Jane		work in a hospital	visit family

		Student B	
	Now	**Every Monday Morning**	**Every Saturday Night**
Sally		baby-sit	work at a movie theatre
Sam	read a magazine		go out with friends
John		play tennis	stay home
Jane	take a nap		

Video Activities: Pet Behavior

Before You Watch.

1. Which of these animals are common pets?
    a. dog   b. lion   c. cat   d. chicken

2. What is an animal shelter for?
    a. sick pets   b. bad pets   c. homeless pets

Watch.

1. What was the dog owner's problem?
    a. The dogs ate a lot.
    b. The dogs were noisy.
    c. The dogs destroyed things.

2. What was the dogs' problem?
    a. They were bored.   b. They were afraid.   c. They were hungry.

3. What is Emily's business?
    a. She adopts dogs.   b. She teaches dogs.   c. She visits dogs.

4. What do most dogs need?
    a. other dogs   b. a lot of toys   c. people's attention

5. Everyone who adopts a dog from the animal shelter promises to _____.
    a. spend time with the dog
    b. send the dog to school
    c. hire Emily

Watch Again.

1. What are the dogs' names?
    _____ Weiner   _____ Arnold
    _____ Max   _____ Taylor
    _____ Otis

2. Check the things that the dogs damaged.
    _____ couch   _____ fireplace
    _____ coffee table   _____ curtains
    _____ bed   _____ chair
    _____ carpet   _____ table

After You Watch.   Unscramble the sentences. Put the words in the correct order.

1. usually like dogs people spend to time with

2. often destroy dogs bored things

3. their to owners animals play need with pets

4. hate home dogs be to alone usually

Chapter 4

Health Care

PART 1

Listening to Conversations

Before You Listen

1   **Preparing to Listen.**

Look at the picture.

1. Describe the picture. How does Ali feel?
2. Ali is going to make a phone call. Who do you think he will call?

2   **Vocabulary Preview.**   Ali is talking on the phone.

1. Listen to his conversation. Circle the words and expressions you don't know.

Nouns		**Verb**
the flu	health clinic	to make an appointment
ID card	insurance card / insurance number	

2. Guess the meanings of the underlined words. Write your guess on the lines. Check your answers with a dictionary or your teacher.

1. You can't walk into the doctor's office to see her at any time that you want; you have to see her at a particular time of day, so you have <u>to make an appointment</u> first.

   My guess: _____

2. The university has a <u>health clinic</u>; all the students go there when they are sick.

   My guess: _____

3. When Ali came to the university, he got an <u>ID card</u> with his name, address, photo, and student number on it.

   My guess: _____

4. Ali has a <u>health insurance card</u>. It shows that he can visit the health clinic while he is in college.

   My guess: _____

5. I feel sick: I'm hot and I ache all over. I think that I have <u>the flu</u>.

My guess: _____

Listen

3 **Listening for the Main Idea.** Listen to Ali's conversation. As you listen, answer this question.

Where is Ali going tomorrow?

4 **Listening for Specific Information.** Listen again. This time, answer these questions.

1. Who is Ali calling?
2. When is his appointment?
3. Should Ali bring money to the appointment?
4. What should Ali bring to the appointment?
5. What information does the receptionist ask for?

After You Listen

5 **Discussing Main Ideas.** Work with a partner. Discuss the answers to these questions.

1. What does Ali think that he has?
2. Do you call a doctor when you have the flu? Why or why not?
3. What do you do when you have the flu?

6 **Vocabulary Review.** Complete these sentences. Use words from the list.

ID card	insurance number	the flu
to make an appointment	health clinic	

1. Ali's very sick. He may have _____ _____.

2. Ali wants _____ _____ _____ _____ to see a doctor tomorrow.

3. Here is my _____ _____. It shows my name and address.

4. He's sick. He's going to the _____ _____.

5. He's going to need his health _____ _____ when he goes to the clinic.

Stress

7 **Listening for Stressed Words.** Listen to the first part of the conversation again.

1.   The stressed words are missing. Fill in the blanks with words from the list.

afternoon	flu	like	1 o'clock
appointment	help	money	think
bring	ID	No	tomorrow
card	insurance	Oh	would

Receptionist: Health Clinic. Can I _____ you?

_1_

Ali: Yes. I _____ I have the _____.

_2_   _3_

Receptionist: _____ you _____ to make an _____?

_4_   _5_   _6_

Ali: Yes, I'd like to see a doctor.

Receptionist: All right. Can you come in _____ _____

_7_   _8_

at _____?

_9_

Ali: Yes, I can come then. _____! Should I _____

_10_   _11_

any _____?

_12_

Receptionist: _____ — just your _____ and _____

_13_   _14_   _15_

_____.

_16_

Ali: OK.

2.   Now read the conversation with a partner. Practice stressing words correctly.

Reductions

8 **Comparing Long and Reduced Forms.** Listen to the following sentences from the conversation. They contain reduced forms. Repeat them after the speaker.

| **Long Form** | **Reduced Form** |

1.   <u>Would you</u> like to make an appointment?   <u>Wudja</u> like to make an appointment?

2.   Yes, <u>I would</u> like to see a doctor.   Yes, <u>I'd</u> like to see a doctor.

3.   <u>Could you</u> come in tomorrow afternoon at 1:00?   <u>Cudja</u> come in tomorrow afternoon at 1:00?

4.   <u>We will</u> see <u>you</u> tomorrow at one.   <u>We'll</u> see <u>ya</u> tomorrow at one.

9 Listening for Reductions. Listen and circle the letter of the sentence that you hear. If you hear a reduction*, circle the letter of the reduced sentence, even though it is not a correct written form.

1. a. I would like to make an appointment.
    b. I'd like to make an appointment.

2. a. Would you like to see Dr. Johnson at eleven?
    b. Wudja* like to see Dr. Johnson at eleven?

3. a. Could you make it at one?
    b. Cudja* make it at one?

4. a. All right. We'll see you at one.
    b. All right. We'll see ya* at one.

Talk It Over

If you have a problem, what should you do?

1. Work with a partner. Look at the following problems. Talk about what to do with your partner. Do you agree? If not, why not?
2. Write your solutions in the chart.

	Solution: Student 1	Solution: Student 2
1. You have a bad headache.		
2. Someone steals your bicycle.		
3. You accidentally eat or drink something bad.		
4. You are very sad and upset.		
5. You cut yourself badly.		
6. You have a bad toothache.		
7. There's a fire in your apartment.		

| **PART 2** | # Listening Skills |

Getting Meaning from Context

1 **Vocabulary Preview.**   You are going to hear some telephone calls. Listen to these words and expressions from the phone calls. Circle the ones you don't know.

Nouns		**Verb**	**Adjective**
a cavity	a checkup	to take your temperature	stolen
a (dental) cleaning	an (eye) exam		

2 **Using Context Clues.**   Here is a list of services that you can call when you need help.

1. Read the list and make sure that you understand each one.

    _____ the health clinic   _____ the police department

    _____ the dental clinic   _____ the eye clinic

    _____ the fire department

2. Listen to the telephone calls. The first part of the call is missing.
3. Listen to the question. Who is the speaker calling? Write the number of the call next to the answer in the list of services.
4. Then listen to the next two sentences. They give you the correct answer.
5. Work with a partner. Compare your answers.

Listening to Instructions

Before You Listen

3 **Preparing to Listen.**   Before you listen, talk about illnesses with a partner.

1. Do you ever get sick?
2. What do you do when you are sick?

4 **Vocabulary Preview.**   You are going to hear a conversation at a health clinic. Listen to these words and expressions from the conversation. Circle the ones you don't know.

Nouns		**Verbs**
aspirin	flu	to ache
a cold	fluids	to cough
drugstore	medicine	to sneeze
a fever	prescription	

Listen

5 **Listening for the Main Idea.** Ali is at the health clinic. As you listen to the conversation, answer this question.

What's wrong with Ali?

6 **Listening to Instructions.** Listen again. Cross out the incorrect words in the sentence under each picture.

1. You should (~~go to school~~ / stay in bed) and (~~exercise~~ / rest) as much as possible.

2. You can take (two aspirin / four aspirin) (four times / two times) a day. That will help the fever and the aches and pains.

3. Be sure to (drink plenty of fluids / eat plenty of fruits). Fruit juice and (coffee / hot tea) are the best.

4. Here's a prescription for some (cold / cough) medicine. You can take it to any (department store / drugstore.)

5. Take your medicine (when you feel bad / with your meals) because it might (upset your stomach / upset your mother).

After You Listen

7 **Discussing Your Opinion.** In small groups, discuss the answers to these questions.

1. Talk about home remedies (things you make at home to feel better; a doctor does not usually prescribe them). Do you use any when you get sick?

2. In your opinion, do herbal remedies (remedies that come from plants) work very well for colds and the flu? Which ones? How do they help?

Listening to Complaints

Before You Listen

8 Preparing to Listen. You are going to hear several people complain about their illnesses. Before you listen, discuss this question.

    Which illnesses and other problems can cause pain?

9 Vocabulary Preview. Listen. Circle the words and phrases you don't know.

Nouns		**Verbs**
ankle	a cavity	to break (a leg)
bandage	headache	to go around (an illness)
broken bone		to sprain (an ankle)
		to vomit

Listen

10 Listening for Main Ideas. As you listen to the complaints, answer these questions.

1. How many speakers are there?
2. How many speakers say that they are in pain?
3. What kind of pain do they have?

11 Listening to Complaints. Listen again. Choose one of the following statements as advice for each person. Write the number of the speaker next to the best advice.

_____ You should take two aspirin for the pain and see a dentist as soon as possible.

_____ You should wrap a tight bandage around your ankle. Don't walk on it for a few days.

_____ You can take some medicine from the drugstore for the sneezing and coughing. Drink plenty of fluids and try to rest.

_____ You should take two aspirin. See a doctor if your head still hurts tomorrow.

_____ You must go to a doctor a get a cast put on your leg.

_____ You shouldn't eat anything for two or three hours—until you stop vomiting. Then you can have clear fluids. If that doesn't work, see a doctor.

After You Listen

12 Discussing Complaints. Work with a partner. Discuss the complaints in Activity 11. Compare your answers. Did you give the same advice? What are some other remedies for each complaint?

PART 3

Reading

Before You Read

1   **Vocabulary Preview.**   Sometimes we can make an adjective from a noun by adding a *y* to the singular form of the noun. For example, to change the noun *rain* into an adjective, we add a *y*—*rainy*—this means "there's a lot of rain." Complete the following sentences with the appropriate adjective.

1.   If something has a lot of dirt, it's _____*dirty*_____ .

2.   If you have a lot of <u>luck</u>, you are _____.

3.   If there's a lot of <u>wind</u>, it's _____.

4.   If there are a lot of <u>rocks</u> on the beach, it is _____.

5.   If you need a lot of <u>sleep</u>, you are _____.

2   **Making Good Guesses.**   Remember that sometimes you can understand new words without a dictionary. For example, you can figure out or guess the meaning from other words in the sentence. Guess the meaning of the underlined words. Circle the letter to complete the sentence.

1.   People who are <u>sleep-deprived</u> are always tired, often get angry easily, and don't do as well as other people on tests.
     Sleep-deprived most likely means ___ .
     a.   having a lot of sleep
     b.   getting angry easily
     c.   not having enough sleep

2.   He fell asleep and died in a terrible car <u>crash</u>.
     Crash most likely means ____.
     a.   a long trip
     b.   an accident
     c.   a small problem

3.   George liked <u>mental</u> work, but not physical work. He liked to do math problems, but he hated to work in the garden.
     Mental most likely means ____.
     a.   in your mind
     b.   with your body
     c.   paying a lot of money

4. Last week we worked 30 hours. This week the company <u>increased</u> our work hours to 40.

   Increased most likely means _____.

   a.   make something smaller
   b.   stop doing something
   c.   make something larger

5. He started working when he was 10. He worked hard all his life. He is <u>used to</u> hard work. "I like hard work," he says.

   When you are *used to* something, most likely you _____.

   a.   know a lot about it and it is familiar
   b.   don't know anything about it and it is new
   c.   know something about it but you don't like it

6. When a government spends more money than it receives, it has a <u>deficit</u>. The government must try to eliminate the deficit.

   The word *deficit* most likely means _____.

   a.   taxes
   b.   money from a government
   c.   spending without enough money

Read

3   Read the article. Don't use your dictionary. If you don't know some words, try to guess their meaning.

Sleep and Health

A | One of the easiest and cheapest ways to help your health is just to sleep eight hours or more every night, but more and more people in the world are not sleeping enough. According to the World Health Organization, over half the people in the world may be sleep-deprived. The result of this is not just a lot of tired people; in the US alone, sleepy drivers cause at least 100,000 car crashes and 1,500 deaths a year. Problems with sleep can also cause mental problems, as well as medical problems such as high blood pressure, diabetes, thyroid problems, and heart problems.

B | "Anything that slows down work is a waste," said Thomas Edison, the inventor of the light bulb. After the invention of the light bulb, he predicted that work days could be increased to 24 hours a day. American culture values work and often doesn't value sleep; in fact, people who sleep a lot are often called "lazy." Many famous business and political leaders say proudly, "I only have time to sleep 4 or 5 hours a night." Students, especially college students, often sleep only a few hours a night. They often say, "I'm used to sleeping only a little."

C | But, according to experts, sleep is like money. If you sleep only 5 hours a day, you don't "get used to it," but instead, build up a "sleep deficit." "It's like a credit card," says Dr. James Maas, the author of *Power Sleep*. "You are only borrowing time. You always have to pay it back." The more hours you don't sleep, the more hours you should sleep to "pay back" the hours on your "sleep credit card." For example, if you sleep 4 hours on Monday and then sleep 8 hours on Tuesday, on Wednesday you will still have a "sleep deficit" of 4 hours. This deficit can continue for months or even years. People with a "sleep deficit" are sleep-deprived; driving and making decisions can be dangerous for these people.

D | Stanley Coren's research showed that when people sleep 10 hours, they do better on tests of mental ability and mood. Research also shows that when people sleep in special rooms without clocks or windows, they usually sleep 9 or 10 hours. This probably means most people should sleep 9 or 10 hours every night. If this is true, even more than half the people in the world may be running a "sleep deficit." You didn't do your homework last night? Maybe you can tell your teacher that you were working hard on your sleep deficit.

E | Winston Churchill, the famous leader of England during World War II, worked late at night, but he also often took naps (short sleeps) during the day. He knew sleep was important. He once said, "Don't think you will be doing less work because you sleep during the day. That's a foolish idea held by people who have no imagination. You will be able to do more."

Cross-Cultural Note

In English we say "time is money." When we talk about time and money, we often use the same verbs. For example, we "spend" time, and we "spend" money. We "waste" time, and we "waste" money. We "save" time, and we "save" money. Does your language have this pattern? In your culture do people talk about time and money with the same words in your language?

After You Read

4 **Finding the Main Ideas.** Circle the letter of the main idea of "Sleep and Health."

a. Sleepy drivers are dangerous.
b. Students should do their homework.
c. Getting enough sleep is very important.
d. Anything that slows down work is a waste.

Read the story again. Match the following main ideas with the correct paragraphs. Write the letter (A, B, C, D, or E) of each paragraph in the appropriate blank.

____B____ American culture values working more than sleeping.

_____ Sleep deprivation is a big problem.

_____ This paragraph really says "good-bye" to the reader.

_____ People may need 9 or 10 hours of sleep.

_____ When you don't sleep enough, you need to sleep more later.

Discussing the Reading

5 Discuss the following questions in small groups.

1. How many hours do you sleep every night?
2. Do you ever feel tired?

<table>
<tr><td>**PART 4**</td><td># Writing</td></tr>
</table>

Using Sentence Patterns

Sentence Pattern 5.   Read the information and examine the sentence patterns in the box. Then do the exercise that follows.

subject	+	modal	+	simple form of verb
He		should		study.
I		will		work.
People		are going to		complain.
You		have to		go.

The modals add the opinion of the speaker or writer. *Should* adds "I think it is a good idea or the correct thing to do." *Will* adds "I believe it is definitely going to happen in the future." *Be going to* adds "this action is in the future." *Have to* adds "This action is necessary or required."

The article "Sleep and Health" uses the modal *should* three times. Underline the three sentences in the article.

We often use the modal *should* to give advice. Write one piece of advice about each of the following ideas. Remember to use the simple form of the verb.

Example: To be healthy ___you should exercise._____

1. To have money _____

2. To have friends _____

3. To learn English _____

4. To be happy _____

Now work with your classmates. Read aloud your pieces of advice from the previous exercise. Write down two other pieces of advice for each topic.

1. To have money _____

    _____

2. To have friends _____

    _____

3. To learn English _____

    _____

4. To be happy _____

    _____

Here is a student's answer to the question, "Should education be free in this country?" It is a simple opinion paragraph. Read the paragraph and the information that follows.

Education should be free in this country for several good reasons. First, it is the fair thing to do. All people should have a chance for an education. Second, education is good for the country. A country is strong if everyone has a good education. Third, free education helps people's health. When people have a good education, they will exercise, stop smoking, and eat more healthy foods. For these reasons, education should be free in this country.

A typical outline for paragraphs in academic writing is:

1. Topic Sentence: statement of opinion
   a. reason number 1 + explanation (supporting statement)
   b. reason number 2 + explanation (supporting statement)
   c. reason number 3 + explanation (supporting statement)
2. Conclusion: summary

Look at the opinion paragraph again. There are eight sentences. Match the sentences to the following outline. Write each sentence in the appropriate blank.

1. Topic Sentence: statement of opinion

   Education should be free in this country for several good reasons.

   a. reason number 1

      _____

      + explanation (supporting statement)

      _____

   b. reason number 2

      _____

      + explanation (supporting statement)

      _____

   c. reason number 3

      _____

      + explanation (supporting statement)

      _____

2. Conclusion: summary

   _____

Practicing the Writing Process

1   **Exploring Ideas: Brainstorming and Free Writing.**   You are going to write an opinion paragraph that answers this question: Should tobacco be illegal (against the law)? Sometimes you can get ideas by brainstorming on your own, for example, when you freewrite. Other times it's good to work with a group or the whole class and get ideas together. In a group or as a class, make a list of reasons tobacco should be made illegal and reasons tobacco shouldn't be made illegal. On separate paper, write down ideas for both sides of the argument.

Now decide which side you are on. Think about your argument and freewrite your ideas. Work with a partner. Read aloud your ideas. Then discuss them with your partner.

2   **Writing the First Draft.**   Write a first draft of your paragraph. Begin with "This country should make tobacco illegal" or "This country shouldn't make tobacco illegal." When necessary, use modals from the list on page 80.

3   **Editing.**   Check your opinion paragraph. Use the following checklist to correct any mistakes.

Editing Checklist

1.   Are the verbs used with modals in the simple form (*study, work, discover, go*)?

2.   Are the modals correct (*should* if you think something is a good idea or the correct thing to do, *will* if you believe something is definitely going to happen in the future, etc.)?

3.   Do your sentences begin with capital letters?

4.   Do other words in the writing need capital letters?

5.   Do your sentences end with periods?

4   **Peer Editing.**   Show your paragraph to another student. Read each other's paragraphs. Does your partner's paragraph have a topic sentence, interesting reasons and explanations, a conclusion? Use the Editing Checklist to check your classmate's paragraph.

5   **Writing the Second Draft.**   Write your second draft and give it to your teacher.

PART 5

Grammar

A. Modal Auxiliaries: Expressing Present Abilities—*Can* and *Can't* (*Cannot*)

The modal auxiliaries are *can, could, may, might, must, ought to, shall, should, will,* and *would*. These are special verb forms in English. They do not change forms; they do not add *-s* or *-ed*. They change meaning. Each word has several different meanings.

Affirmative	Negative
I / You / He / She / It / We / You / They } **can run** fast.	I / You / He / She / It / We / You / They } **can't swim.** **cannot swim.**

Notes: Can and *can't (cannot)* are used to tell about abilities. The simple form of a verb always follows *can, can't,* and other modal auxiliaries.

1 Talk about abilities. Make sentences with *can* or *can't*.

Example: swim   I can swim.
                or   I can't swim.

1. run a mile
2. do aerobics
3. play soccer
4. ski
5. play volleyball
6. play tennis
7. lift weights
8. skate
9. play baseball
10. swim
11. dive
12. play basketball

B. *Can:* Yes / No Questions and Short Answers

Yes / No Questions	Possible Answers	
	Affirmative	Negative
Can { I / you / he / she / it we / you / they } **swim** here?	Yes, { I / you / he / she / it we / you / they } **can.**	No, { I / you / she / he / it we / you / they } **can't.**

2 Use *can* to make questions. Take turns asking and answering the questions.

Example: walk ten miles   A: Can you walk ten miles?
                                B: Yes, I can. or No, I can't.

1. touch your toes
2. write poetry
3. run a mile
4. play the piano
5. dance the tango
6. paint a picture
7. do six push-ups
8. sing well
9. water ski
10. whistle
11. _____
12. _____

C. *Can:* Questions with *When, Where,* and *How*

Information Questions			Possible Answers
When can	we	**swim** here?	After 4:30.
Where can	he	**buy** a bicycle?	At City Sports Store.
How far / fast / long can	you	**run?**	For 3 miles / not very fast / for an hour.

Note: How far...? asks about distance. *How fast...?* asks about speed. *How long...?* asks about length or period of time. *For* + period of time is often used in answers.

3   **Information Gap.**   Use question words and *can I* to make questions using these cues. Then take turns asking and answering the questions.
- Student A should cover up Student B's answers.
- Student B should cover up Student A's questions.

Example: where / play tennis at the high school
> A: Where can I play tennis for free?
> B: You can play tennis for free at the high school.

Student A	Student B
1. where / buy running shoes	at any shoe store
2. where / play basketball	at the high school
3. when / use the swimming pool	from 7:00 A.M. to 7:00 P.M.
4. where / rent a bicycle	at a bike shop
5. when / go to aerobics class	at 6:00 P.M.
6. how / learn to dive	take lessons
7. where / buy a basketball	at the sports store
8. where / play volleyball	at the beach
9. how / skate	practice a lot
10. where / surf	in Hawaii

D. Making Requests with *Could*

Questions	Possible Answers		Notes
	Affirmative	**Negative**	
Could I open the window?	Certainly / Sure.	Sorry, it's not possible.	*Could I...*is a polite way to ask someone to allow you to do something.
Could you help me, please?	Yes, of course.	Sorry, but I can't.	In these cases, we are asking someone else to do something.
Could they help me?	No problem!	No, they are busy.	

4   Use *could you* or *could I* to make requests. Use answers from the chart on page 84.

Example: find some aspirin
 A: Could you find some aspirin, please?
 B: No problem!

1. ask you a question
2. help me, please
3. get some information from you
4. fill this prescription for me
5. explain these instructions
6. have some water please
7. give me a bigger bottle
8. recommend something for mosquito bites

E. Expressing Desires and Making Requests with *Would like*

Statements with Nouns	Statements with Infinitives	Notes
Subject + *would like* + **noun**	**Subject** + *would like* + **infinitive**	*Would like* is used to tell our desires and to make polite requests. It is more polite than *want to*.
I would like some aspirin. **I'd** also **like** some cold medicine.	We **would like to buy** some aspirin, please. **We'd** also **like to get** some cold medicine.	The contracted form of *would* is *'d*.

Questions	Possible Answers	
	Affirmative	**Negative**
Would you like some dinner?	Yes, please.	No, thank you.
Would you like to go out for lunch?	Yes, of course.	Sorry, but I can't today.

5   Work with a partner. Ask and answer questions. Use *would you like to...?* with the following cues. Give true answers.

Example: learn CPR (cardiopulmonary resuscitation)
 A: Would you like to learn CPR?
 B: Yes, it's very important.

1. change your eating habits
2. learn first aid
3. take herbs as medicine
4. make an appointment
5. get a massage
6. exercise more often
7. eat healthier food, like vegetables
8. lose some weight

6   **Making Requests.**   Role-play these telephone conversations. Then create your own.

1. You have a bad toothache, and you would like to make an emergency appointment with the dentist. Call the dentist's office.
2. You need a prescription for antibiotics. Ask the pharmacist.
3. Your back hurts. Call the chiropractor for an appointment.
4. You want a massage. Call the spa for an appointment.
5. You want to get in shape. Ask the trainer at the gym for help.

F. Expressing Needs or Obligations with *Have to* and *Must*

	Examples	Notes
have to	I / You / We / They **have to use** a car seat with small children. He / She / It **has to sit** in a car seat.	*Have to* and *must* are very similar in meaning. They show that something is very important or necessary
must	I / You / He / She / It / We / They **must use** a car seat with small children.	

7   Use the cues below to make sentences with *have to*, *has to*, or *must*.

Example: He / buy a car seat for his daughter.
> He has to buy a car seat for his daughter.
> or He must buy a car seat for his daughter.

1. You / obey the speed limit.
2. The landlord / keep the building clean.
3. Children / have immunizations
4. Kathy / go to the dentist
5. I / visit my grandmother

G. Future Tense with *Will*: Affirmative and Negative Statements

Affirmative		Negative	
I / You / She / He / It We / You / They	**will be** here soon.	I / You / She / He / It We / You / They	**will not be** late. **won't be**

Note: Will is used to talk about the future. People also use *will* to make offers, predictions, promises, and requests.

8   We often use *will* or *won't* to make promises. Imagine you are going away from home for the first time. You are talking to your parents. Use the following cues to make promises with *will* or *won't*. Then add two more promises.

Example: eat healthy food
        I promise I will eat healthy food, Mom.

1. eat breakfast every day _____

2. get a lot of sleep _____

3. not go to many parties _____

4. get some exercise every week _____

5. not watch soap operas _____

6. read more books _____

7. do the laundry _____

8. not call collect _____

9. _____

10. _____

H. Future Tense with *Will*: Questions and Answers

Statement	She will study for the test	
Yes / No questions	***Will* + subject + verb** **Will** she **study** for the test?	Yes, she will. No, she won't.
Information questions	**Question word +** *will* **+ subject + verb** **When** **will** she **study?** **Where** **will** she **study?**	Tonight. At home.

9   People often use *will* to make requests. Imagine you and your partner are very good friends. Both of you are moving to new places, and you are saying good-bye. Take turns making requests and giving responses. Use the cues below and add two original requests.

Example: write soon
        A: Will you write soon?
        B: Of course. I promise I will.

1. call me from time to time
2. take care of yourself
3. have a good time
4. be careful

5. remember all of us
6. keep in touch
7. _____
8. _____

Video Activities: Brain Surgery

Before You Watch.

1. When a doctor has to fix a heart, what does he or she do?
   a. an examination   b. a transplant   c. surgery

2. What part of your body controls movement?
   a. your eyes   b. your heart   c. your brain   d. your leg

Watch.

1. What is this a picture of?
   a. a brain
   b. a heart
   c. a hand

2. Check the ways that Dr. Francel's surgery is different from other surgeries.

   _____ It's faster.   _____ He uses computers.
   _____ It's cheaper.   _____ He operates on brains.

3. Before the surgery, Mr. Previt's hand _____.
   a. hurts   b. cannot move   c. shakes

4. During the surgery, Mr. Previt is _____.
   a. sleeping   b. awake   c. shaking

5. After the surgery, Mr. Previt _____.
   a. can hold a glass   b. cannot feel his hand   c. can talk better

Watch Again.   Complete the sentences with numbers from the box.

$1\frac{1}{2}$ to 2	12	100	2

1. Dr. Francel does this surgery in _____ hours.
2. Other doctors do this surgery in _____ hours.
3. Dr. Francel can operate on _____ patients in a day.
4. A human hair is about _____ microns thick.

After You Watch.   Complete the sentences with the correct modal.

1. Dr. Francel _____ operate very quickly.
         can   should   must
2. All doctors _____ use computers.
         should   have to   would
3. Dr. Francel's surgery _____ take less time than in other hospitals.
         might   must   will
4. A brain surgeon _____ work very carefully.
         has to   might   could
5. If a surgeon is not careful, his patient _____ die.
         must   can't   might

Chapter 5

Men and Women

Listening to Conversations

Before You Listen

1   **Preparing to Listen.**

Describe the picture of Beth and
her friend Michel.

2   **Vocabulary Preview.**   Alicia and Lee are at Beth's apartment. Beth is on the phone.

1.   Listen to these words from their conversation. Circle the ones you don't know.

Nouns	Adjectives	Verbs
matchmaker	cross-cultural	ask (someone) out
permission	strict	date / make a date with (someone)
		go out with

2.   Guess the meanings of the underlined words. Write your guess on the lines.
     Check your answers with a dictionary or your teacher.

1.   David is going to <u>ask</u> Jennifer <u>out.</u> He's calling her right now to ask her
     to go to the movies.
     My guess: _____

2.   Many children need <u>permission</u> before they can take snacks from the
     refrigerator. Other parents, however, let children have snacks whenever
     they want.
     My guess: _____

3.   Nabil and Mary have a <u>cross-cultural</u> marriage: he's from Egypt and
     she's from Canada.
     My guess: _____

4.   Beth is <u>dating</u> Michel. They go to the movies or to concerts together
     almost every weekend.
     My guess: _____

5. Alicia's parents are <u>strict.</u> They have a lot of rules about how they want her to behave.

    My guess: _____

6. Some cultures have <u>matchmakers</u> to help people find someone to marry.

    My guess: _____

Listen

3 **Listening for the Main Idea.**   Listen to the conversation. As you listen, answer this question.

> What are Alicia, Beth, and Lee talking about?

4 **Listening for Specific Information.**   Listen again. This time answer these questions.

1. Who is Beth talking to on the phone?
2. Where did Beth meet Michel?
3. Who does Alicia want Lee to meet?
4. What is Lee going to do?

After You Listen

5 **Discussing Main Ideas.**   Work with a partner. Discuss the answers to these questions.

1. According to Beth, is Michel her boyfriend? What does she say about this?
2. Is it easy for Alicia to go on a date with a boy? Why or why not?
3. How is dating in Korea different today from the past?

6 **Vocabulary Review.**   Complete these sentences. Use words from the list.

matchmaker	ask (someone) out	go out with
make a date	cross-cultural	permission

1. Alicia can't go out with a boy unless she has her parents' _____.

2. Alicia is like a _____ because she is trying to find a girlfriend for Lee.

3. Beth is going to _____ _____ _____ Michel tomorrow night.

4. Beth's parents have a _____ marriage: her father is American and her mother is from Italy.

5. Lee decided to _____ _____ _____ with Alicia's classmate. He invited her to dinner this weekend.

6. Lee's parents only want Lee to _____ Korean girls _____ on dates.

Stress

7   **Listening for Stressed Words.**   Listen to the first part of the conversation again.

1.   The stressed words are missing. Fill in the blanks with words from the list. Some words may be used more than once.

accepted	date	out	that
asked	Mexico	parents'	tomorrow
boy	Michel	7 o'clock	yet
boyfriend (two times)	one	special	

Beth: OK, great! I'll see you _____ at _____. Right. Bye!
           ₁   ₂

Alicia: Hmm. Who was _____?
                            ₃

Lee: Yeah! Someone _____?
                          ₄

Beth: That was _____, a really nice guy in my computer science class.
                     ₅

           He _____ me _____. I _____, so…
              ₆   ₇   ₈

Alicia: So, _____ phone call, and now you have a _____!
                  ₉   ₁₀

Beth: Oh, c'mon, Alicia. He's not my _____ — _____!
                                          ₁₁   ₁₂

Alicia: Well, it sounds nice. In _____, I needed my _____
                                      ₁₃   ₁₄

           permission to go out on a _____ with a _____.
                                      ₁₅   ₁₆

2.   Now read the conversation with a partner. Practice stressing words correctly.

Reductions

8   **Comparing Long and Reduced Forms.**   Listen to these examples of reductions. Notice that *did you* after *What, When, Where, Who, Why,* and *How* reduces to /jə/.

Long Form	**Reduced Form**
1. Where <u>did you</u> go last night?	Where <u>ja</u> go last night?
2. Who <u>did you</u> go with?	Who <u>ja</u> go with?
3. What <u>did you</u> see at the movies?	Who <u>ja</u> see at the movies?
4. How <u>did you</u> get there?	How <u>ja</u> get there?
5. When <u>did you</u> get home?	When <u>ja</u> get home?
6. Why <u>did you</u> pick that movie?	Why <u>ja</u> pick that movie?

9 **Listening for Reductions.** Listen and circle the letter of the sentence that you hear. If you hear a reduction*, circle the letter of the reduced sentence, even though it is not a correct written form.

1. a. What did you do last weekend?
   b. What ja* do last weekend?

2. a. Where did you go on Sunday?
   b. Where ja* go on Sunday?

3. a. When did you get up this morning?
   b. When ja* get up this morning?

4. a. How did you get to school?
   b. How ja* get to school?

5. a. Who did you come to school with?
   b. Who ja* come to school with?

6. a. Why did you take the bus?
   b. Why ja* take the bus?

Talk It Over

What do your classmates think about dating etiquette (rules of behavior)?

1. Write the names of your group members in the spaces at the top of the chart.
2. Ask your group members about dating etiquette. Write their answers on the chart.
3. Then discuss your answers.

Questions	Name _____	Name _____	Name _____	Name _____
1. It's OK for someone to ask a stranger for a date.	_____ Yes _____ No	_____ Yes _____ No	_____ Yes _____ No	_____ Yes _____ No
2. You shouldn't ask someone for a date unless you have been formally introduced to that person.	_____ Yes _____ No	_____ Yes _____ No	_____ Yes _____ No	_____ Yes _____ No
3. You should ask someone for a date at least three days before you want to go out.	_____ Yes _____ No	_____ Yes _____ No	_____ Yes _____ No	_____ Yes _____ No
4. It's OK for a woman to ask a man out for a date.	_____ Yes _____ No	_____ Yes _____ No	_____ Yes _____ No	_____ Yes _____ No
5. It's OK for the woman to pay for the date.	_____ Yes _____ No	_____ Yes _____ No	_____ Yes _____ No	_____ Yes _____ No
6. If you go to a restaurant on a date and the other person is paying, you shouldn't order the most expensive item on the menu.	_____ Yes _____ No	_____ Yes _____ No	_____ Yes _____ No	_____ Yes _____ No
7. After a first date, you shouldn't tell the person that you'd like to see him or her again unless it's the truth.	_____ Yes _____ No	_____ Yes _____ No	_____ Yes _____ No	_____ Yes _____ No

| PART 2 | # Listening Skills |

Getting Meaning from Context

1 **Vocabulary Preview.**   You are going to hear some conversations. Listen to these words and expressions from the conversations. Circle the ones you don't know.

Nouns	**Verb**	**Adjectives**
date	get in	modern
student ticket		terrible

2 **Using Context Clues.**

1. Listen to the first part of each conversation.
2. Listen to the question and circle the letter of the best answer.
3. Then listen to the last part to hear the correct answer.

  1. What did Beth do on her date?
      a.   She had a pizza and then saw a movie.
      b.   She went to the movies.
      c.   She saw a movie and then went to a restaurant.
  2. Why is Jennifer upset?
      a.   The traffic was terrible.
      b.   Rob was late for their date.
      c.   Rob forgot their date.
  3. What is Dina probably going to do?
      a.   Go out with Ali on Friday night.
      b.   Go out with Ali some other night.
      c.   Not go out with Ali.
  4. What is Pat probably going to do?
      a.   Go out with Ali on Friday night.
      b.   Go out with Ali some other night.
      c.   Not go out with Ali.
  5. Why can't Lee go to the concert?
      a.   He doesn't have enough money.
      b.   He's doing something else on Saturday.
      c.   The concert is too late.

3 **Discussing Dates.**   Work with a partner. Discuss the answers to these questions.

1. What is a typical date for you?
2. What is your idea of a fun date?

Listening to Invitations

Before You Listen

4 **Preparing to Listen.**   Before you listen, talk about invitations with a partner.

1. Do you ever invite friends to your house for dinner?
2. Do you ever invite friends to your house to watch a movie?
3. Do you like formal or informal dinners?

5 **Vocabulary Preview.**   Listen. Circle the words and expressions you don't know.

Verbs	**Adjectives**
have someone (over) for dinner	formal
have something under control	informal
invite someone (over)	

Listen

6 **Listening for Main Ideas.**   Beth is inviting Michel to dinner. As you listen to her invitation, answer these questions.

1. What time is Beth's dinner?
2. Is the dinner formal or informal?
3. Is Michel going to come?
4. Does Beth want Michel to bring something?

7 **Listening to Invitations.**   Listen again. Look at the pictures and circle the words that you hear.

After You Listen

8 **Discussing Dinner Parties.** Compare your answers for Activity 7 with a partner. Do you have the same words? Then talk in small groups about the answers to these questions.

- ◼ In your community, do guests offer to bring food or drinks to a dinner party?
- ◼ When you go to dinner at someone's house, do you bring a gift?

Listening to Responses

Before You Listen

9 **Preparing to Listen.** In small groups, talk about accepting and refusing invitations.

1. What do you say when you want to accept an invitation?
2. What do you say when you can't accept an invitation?
3. What do you say when you don't want to accept an invitation?

10 **Vocabulary Preview.** Listen. Circle the words and expressions you don't know.

Verbs	**Adjectives**	**Expression**
accept an invitation	apologetic	some other time
play (a game)	bored	
	excited	

Listen

11 **Listening for Main Ideas.** David is talking to Ali and Beth. He wants them to do something special with him. As you listen, answer these questions.

1. Where does David want to go on Friday night?
2. Who wants to go with him?

12 **Listening to Responses.** Listen again. Choose the best answer to each question.

1. How does David feel?
   a. excited
   b. bored
   c. apologetic

2. How does Beth feel?
   a. excited
   b. bored
   c. apologetic

3. How does Ali feel?
   a. excited
   b. bored
   c. apologetic

After You Listen

13 **Discussing Invitations.** Answer the following questions in small groups.

1. How do you feel when you can't accept an invitation?
2. Do people always tell the truth when they can't accept an invitation? Why or why not?
3. Do you always tell the truth when you can't accept an invitation?

PART 3	# Reading

Before You Read

Picture 1

Picture 2

1 Look at the pictures and read what the people say. Then answer and discuss the following questions with a partner or in small groups.

1. In Picture 1, the man doesn't understand something. What is it?
2. In Picture 1, the woman is a little angry. Why?
3. In Picture 2, the woman is unhappy. Why?
4. In Picture 2, the man is unhappy. Why?
5. Do men and women talk in different ways?

2 **Vocabulary Preview.**   Sometimes you can understand a new word because the meaning is after the phrase "in other words."

Example: The scientist had a good <u>imagination</u>; in other words, he thought of new, creative ideas easily.
You use your imagination to *think up new, creative ideas.*

Write the definition (meaning) of the following underlined words. Look for the meaning after the phrase "in other words."

1. My twin brothers are very <u>similar</u>. In other words, they like the same things and play in the same way. They aren't very different.

    Similar means not _____

2. Boys <u>brag</u>; in other words, they say good things about themselves.

    When people *brag*, they say _____

3. Little boys are usually <u>active</u>; in other words, they do things.

    Active people don't sit and do nothing. They _____

We can often guess the meaning of a word from the words around it—the context. Use the context of the following sentences to understand the five words in the exercise that follows. Then match the words with the definitions. Do not use your dictionary.

1. I apologized to my wife. I said, "I'm really sorry about last night."
2. My boss gives me orders all the time. He says, "copy this," or "get the mail," or "make coffee." I don't like it.
3. He has a high position in the company. Everyone thinks he will be president some day.
4. I have a good suggestion: I think we should have some lunch now.
5. We are equal in the company. We have exactly the same position.

1. __b__ apologize
2. _____ orders
3. _____ position
4. _____ suggestions
5. _____ equal

a. ideas ("Maybe we should do this.")
b. to say "I'm sorry"
c. commands ("Do this.")
d. same
e. place in a group ("president")

Read

3   Read the following article. Don't use a dictionary. Instead use the diagrams, examples, and words in parentheses to understand new words. Also remember you can find the meaning of a new word after the phrase "in other words."

Men's Talk and Women's Talk in the United States

A   Marriage often is not easy. Love often is not easy. Sometimes friendship between a man and a woman is not easy. Maybe a man and a woman love or like each other, but they argue. They get angry. Later they apologize, but it happens again and again. What's the problem? Are men and women really very different?

B   Deborah Tannen says yes. Men and women are very different. Tannen teaches at Georgetown University. She writes books about the ways people talk. She believes that men and women talk—and think—in different ways. She tells about some differences in her book "You Just Don't Understand."

C   The differences, Tannen says, begin when men and women are children. Very young boys and girls are similar to each other. In other words, they like the same things and play in the same ways. They aren't very different. But then there is a change.

D   When children in the United States are five or six years old, boys usually play in large groups. One boy gives orders. For example, he says, "Take this," "Go over there," and "Be on this team." He is the leader. Boys also brag. In other words, they say good things about themselves. They do this to have a high position. Position in the group is important to boys.

high position

low position

E   Girls in the United States usually play in small groups or with one other girl. A girl's "best friend"—her very, very good friend—is important to her. Girls don't often give orders; they give suggestions. For example, they say, "Let's go over there," "Maybe we should do this," and "Do you want to play with that?" Girls don't usually have a leader, and they don't often brag. Everyone has an equal position.

equal positions   ←——————→

F   Little boys are usually active; they do things. Much of the time, little girls sit together and talk. When children grow up, nothing really changes. Men usually do things together. Or they talk about activities such as sports and things such as cars and world problems. They talk to give or get information. But for women, people and feelings are important. Women often talk to show interest and love. Although a man and a woman speak the same language, sometimes they don't understand each other. Men's talk and women's talk are almost two different languages. But maybe men and women can learn to understand each other if they understand the differences in speech.

After You Read

4 **Finding the Main Ideas.** Which sentences from the article are about men? Which sentences are about women? Write M (men) or W (women) on each line.

_____M_____ 1. When they are children, they usually play in large groups.

_____ 2. When they are children, they usually play in small groups or with one friend.

_____ 3. There usually isn't a leader in the children's play group.

_____ 4. One child in the play group is the leader.

_____ 5. They talk to show interest and love.

_____ 6. They talk to give or get information.

5 Remember a synopsis gives the information of a text in a very short way. Here are three synopses of the article you just read. None of them is wrong—they all have information from the article. But remember, the best synopsis needs to give <u>all</u> the important information. Choose the best one, then compare your answer with a partner's.

A. Marriage is not easy. Men and women may argue. They may apologize later. This problem can happen many times. Men and women can learn to understand each other if they listen to each other.

B. Men and women talk and think differently. These differences begin as children. Men often talk to give or get information. Women often talk to show interest and love. These differences can cause problems.

C. Deborah Tannen teaches at Georgetown University. She is a writer. She writes about how people talk. She says that men and women are different. She wrote a book called *You Just Don't Understand.*

Discussing the Reading

6 Talk with a small group about your answers to the following questions.

1. When you were a child, did you play in a big group or a small group? Did you have a best friend?
2. Would you like to have a high position in a group, or would you like to be in a group with equal positions?
3. What do you sometimes argue about with your husband? Wife? Boyfriend? Girlfriend?
4. In your country, do men and women talk differently? If so, give examples.

PART 4

Writing

Using Sentence Patterns

Sentence Pattern 6.   Read the information and examine the sentence patterns. Then do the exercises that follow.

We learned that some verbs have an actor, an action, and a receiver of the action—*The car hit the tree*. These are called transitive verbs. We also learned that some verbs have only an actor and an action—*The man jumped*. These are called intransitive verbs. A few verbs describe an action that has an actor and two different receivers—often called the *direct object* and the *indirect object*.

subject +	verb +	indirect object +	direct object
(person)	(thing)		
I	told	Sally	the story.
John	gave	me	some money.
The teacher	asked	Kim	a question.
The waiter	brought	him	a soft drink.

Many of these verbs, for example, *bring*, can also be used with only a direct object or with both a direct object and an indirect object.

Example: He brought lunch.
              He brought me lunch.

Use the following verbs in sentences. On the first blank, write a sentence with only a direct object. On the second blank, write a sentence with both a direct object and an indirect object. Make sure the indirect object comes <u>before</u> the direct object.

1. send: _____

   _____

2. pay: _____

   _____

3. sell: _____

   _____

4. ask: _____

   _____

5. get: _____

   _____

6. make: _____

   _____

Here is a picture story about Henry and Sadae. Look at each picture. Then look at the sentences in the box. In the blanks, write the correct sentences for each picture.

1

They met.

2

3

4

5

6

They were angry at each other.
They met.
He asked her to marry him.
They were in love.
They got married.
He never wanted to talk to her about work.

Practicing the Writing Process

A narrative is a story. It tells about a series of actions. Most often the simple past tense is used. Read the student's story about her parents meeting and marrying.

My father met my mother in 1980. They met at a college dance. My father liked my mother right away, but my mother did not like my father. He asked her to go out on a date. She wanted to say no, but she was too polite and so she said yes. On their date they went to the movies and saw *Raging Bull*, a movie starring Robert De Niro. After the movie they talked for a long time; they even argued about the movie (he liked it but she didn't). My mother decided that my father was very intelligent. Then my mother started to become interested in him. Soon they were in love.

1 **Exploring Ideas: Free Writing.**   Write for 10 minutes about how you met someone close to you. Don't worry about spelling or grammar. Then tell a partner about your story. Don't read your freewrite aloud. Use your own words.

2 **Writing the First Draft.**   Write a first draft of your narrative.

3 **Editing.**   Now check your story. Here is a list of things to check for in your narrative.

Editing Checklist

1. Are the verbs you used transitive or intransitive?
2. Do any of the verbs have direct objects? Indirect objects?
3. Both? Are these verbs used correctly?
4. Did you use the simple past tense? (Remember that most often the simple past tense is used in narratives.)
5. Do you have interesting details in your narrative?
6. Do your sentences begin with capital letters?
7. Do other words in the writing need capital letters?
8. Do your sentences end with periods or other final punctuation?

4 **Peer Editing.**   Show your story to another student. Read and discuss each other's work.

5 **Writing the Second Draft.**   Write your second draft and give it to your teacher.

Writing a Journal

6 Write a journal entry about how you met your best friend. Use the simple past tense, transitive and intransitive verbs, and direct and indirect objects if you can.

I'm going to study chemistry. I want to be a chemist.
My sister is going to study medicine. She wants to be a doctor.

PART 5

Grammar

A. Simple Past Tense: *Was* and *Were*

Affirmative	Negative	
	Long Form	**Contraction**
I / she / he / it **was** happy.	I / she / he / it **was not** sad.	I / she / he / it **wasn't** sad.
We / you / they **were** happy.	We / you / they **were not** sad.	We / you / they **weren't** sad.

Note: The verb *be* is different from other verbs in English. Do not use an auxiliary or helping verb to make negative sentences with the verb *be*.

1 Use *was* or *were* to complete these sentences. Use contractions for the negatives.

1. My grandparents _were_ introduced in 1938. They _____ at a dance.

2. My grandmother's name _____ Catherine. My grandfather's _____ Robert.

3. My grandfather _____ a medical student. My grandmother _____ in high school.

4. They _____ (not) from the same city. My grandfather _____ from Philadelphia. My grandmother _____ from New York.

5. They _____ also from different backgrounds. My grandfather's family _____ Scandinavian. My grandmother's _____ from Spain.

6. Even their religion _____ (not) the same.

7. Finally, her family _____ rich. His family _____ poor.

8. To them, these things _____ (not) important. They _____ in love!

Questions	Affirmative	Negative
Was I tired?	Yes, I **was**.	No, I **wasn't**.
Was she / he / it late?	Yes, she / he / it **was**.	No, she / he / it **wasn't**.
Were you / we / they late?	Yes, you / they / we **were**.	No, you / they / we **weren't**.

Note: The verb *be* is different from other verbs in English. Do not use an auxiliary or helping verb to make questions with the verb *be*.

2 Ask and answer these questions about Christine's grandparents from Activity 1.

Example: A: *Were Catherine and Robert introduced at school?*
             B: *No, they weren't.*

1. Was Robert a medical student?
2. Were they from different backgrounds?
3. Was Catherine the same age as Robert?
4. Were they from the same city?
5. Was Robert from Philadelphia?
6. Was Catherine from Los Angeles?
7. Was Catherine a medical student?
8. Were both families rich?

B. Simple Past Tense: Information Questions

Statement	Catherine's parents were from Spain.
Question with *who*	***Who* + *was* + adjective, noun, or phrase** **Who was** from Spain?
Statement	They were married in New York in 1941.
Question with *when,* *how long, how old*	**Question word + *was* or *were* + subject** **When were** they married? **Where were** they married? **How long** were they married? **How old were** they when they married?

Note: Questions with *who* are normally singular.

3 Make questions from these statements. The answers to the questions are the underlined words.

Examples: Robert was a medical student.   They were introduced in 1938.
   Who was a medical student?   *When were they introduced?*

1. Robert and Catherine were at a dance.
2. Robert was from Philadelphia.
3. Catherine was from New York.
4. She was seventeen.
5. He was twenty-two.
6. Robert's parents were Scandinavian.
7. Her family was from Spain.
8. They were married in 1941.

C. Simple Past Tense: Regular Verbs— Affirmative Statements

Examples	Notes
I / you / he / she / it **worked.** We / you / they **worked.**	The simple past tense is used to talk about actions or situations in the past. This chapter focuses on regular verbs. These verbs use the *-ed* ending.

Note: Some verbs change their spelling when you add *-ed.*

For verbs ending in consonant + *y,* change *y* to *i* and add *-ed: Study — studied; try — tried*

For most verbs ending with one vowel and one consonant, double the final consonant and add *-ed. Hug — hugged; plan — planned*

For some verbs that end in one vowel and one consonant, do not double the final consonant. These are usually verbs that have more than one syllable and do not have stress on the final syllable. Examples are: *entered; happened; ironed; listened; opened; traveled; visited.*

4 Use these pictures and cues to make sentences. Use the past tense of the verbs.

clean	iron	watch	fold
fix	listen to	wash	stay

Example: In the 1950's, most women stayed at home.

D. Simple Past Tense: Negative Statements

Long Form	Contraction
I / he / she / it / you / we / they **did not work**.	I / he / she / it / you / we / they **didn't go**.

5 Read the information about Christine's grandfather. The sentences that follow are not correct. Correct the sentences as in the examples.

Examples: Robert worked in a hospital.
Robert didn't work in a hospital. He worked in a bank.
He was a vice-president.
He wasn't a vice-president. He was a manager.

Name: Robert L. Nathanson
Eye Color: blue
Hair Color: brown
Height: 6'2"
Weight: 210 lbs.
Birth Date: February 15, 1913
Branch of Service: Navy
Length of Service: 1941–1950
Rank: General

Job: Supervisor
Awards: 6 for bravery
Area Served In: New York
Hobbies: Plays tennis

1. He worked in California.
2. He served in the military for six years.
3. He received two awards.
4. He was a captain in the navy.
5. He had brown eyes and blue hair.
6. He played tennis.
7. He weighed 180 pounds.
8. He was 5'10".

E. Simple Past Tense: *Yes / No* Questions and Short Answers

Questions	Short Answers
Did { I / you / she / he / it we / you / they } **work?**	Affirmative: Yes, { I / you / she / he / it we / you / they } **did**. Negative: No, { I / you / she / he / it we / you / they } **didn't**.

6 Read the information about Christine's grandmother. One student uses the eight sentences to make yes / no questions. The other student answers the questions. Then change roles.

Name: Catherine Nathanson
Residence: 2109 Hillside Drive
          Queens, New York
Telephone: 724-0000
Marital Status: Married
Maiden Name: Molina
Children: 2
Eye Color: Brown
Hair Color: Brown
Height: 5'4"
Weight: 110 lbs.

Birth Date: May 28, 1918
Job: Bank Teller
Work Experience: None
Attitude: Works very hard
          enjoys her job

Examples: Catherine lived in New York.
   A: Did Catherine live in New York?
   B: Yes, she did.
   She was married.
   A: Was she single?
   B: No, she wasn't.

1. My grandmother worked in a bank.
2. She had brown hair and blue eyes.
3. She weighed 110 pounds.
4. She had two children.
5. She was born in 1950.
6. She was divorced.
7. Her telephone number was 724-0000.
8. She liked to read.

F. Simple Past Tense: Information Questions

	Examples	Notes
Statement	My father had an accident.	To ask about a subject, use *who* or *what* + past tense verb. Do not use *did* in these questions.
Question with *who*	*Who* + past tense verb **Who** had an accident?	
Statement	An accident happened last night.	
Question with *what*	*What* + past tense verb **What** happened last night?	

Statements	I studied English at the library from eight to ten every night. She studied French with her roommate on weekends.	
Information Questions	**Question word + *did* + subject + verb**	**Possible Answers**
	How often did you **study**? **How long did** you **study**? **What did** you **study**? **Where did** you **When did** she **study**? **What did** she **study**? **Who* did** she **study** with?	Every night Two hours. English. the library. On weekends. French. With her roommate.

*Note: In formal English, *whom* is used for these questions. In spoken English, *who* is more common.

7 Christine's grandfather was in the military for five years. Here is some information about Robert's experience in the navy. For each sentence, make questions about the underlined words.

Example: The U.S. entered the war <u>in 1941</u>.
         When did the U.S. enter the war?

1. <u>My grandfather</u> joined the navy.

2. He was in the navy <u>for five years</u>.

3. He was a <u>captain</u>.

4. He stayed <u>in four different places</u>.

5. He worked in <u>dangerous places</u>.

6. <u>The work</u> was dangerous but important.

7. He enjoyed <u>his work</u>.

8. <u>The navy</u> was terrible.

9. He hated <u>the navy</u>.

10. He missed <u>my grandmother</u>.

11. He wrote to <u>my grandmother</u> almost every night.

12. <u>The war</u> lasted for four long years.

8 **Playing Twenty Questions.**   Pretend you are a famous person from the past. Other students have to guess your name. They can ask you questions in the past tense, but you can only answer yes or no.

Video Activities: Women's Football

Before You Watch.

1. Which of these sports do you like to play or watch?
   a. football   b. soccer   c. basketball   d. tennis
2. Which of the sports above do women usually *not* play?

Watch.

> **Vocabulary Note**
> A professional athlete is a person who gets money for playing a sport.

1. What sport do you see?
   a. soccer   b. football   c. basketball

2. Who is playing?
   a. men   b. women   c. both men and women

3. When did Kim Ketchum begin playing?
   a. in high school   b. a year ago   c. last month
4. Why does she play?
   a.   She wants to make a lot of money.
   b.   She loves the game.
   c.   Her father is a coach.

Watch Again.

1. Check the people that you see or hear at the football game.
   _____ cheerleaders   _____ police   _____ fans
   _____ announcers   _____ doctors   _____ a coach
2. Complete the name of Kim's football team. _____ Vixens
   a. Michigan   b. Minnesota   c. Minneapolis d. Montana
3. Kim's team is part of a football league. What is the abbreviation of its name?
   a. WFL   b. LPFL   c. WPFL
4. How much money has Kim made so far?
   a. $0   b. $100   c. $1,000

After You Watch. Read these sentences about professional basketball player Sheryl Swoopes. Then number them in the correct order.

_____ In 1996, the US team won the gold medal at the Atlanta Olympics.

_____ After the Olympics, Sheryl started playing professional basketball for the Houston Comets.

_____ She played basketball at Texas Tech University.

_____ She graduated from college in 1994.

___1___ At Texas Tech, she scored 1,000 points in 46 games.

_____ Sheryl Swoopes was born in Texas in 1971.

_____ In 1993, she also helped her university team win a National championship.

_____ Then she started playing for the U.S. National Team.

Chapter 6

Sleep and Dreams

Listening to Conversations

Before You Listen

1   **Preparing to Listen.**

Look at this photo.

1.   Where is this student?
2.   What is he doing?
3.   What time of day is it: morning or evening?

2   **Vocabulary Preview.**

Beth and Alicia are at a café. They are drinking coffee. Ali joins them.

1.   Listen to their conversation. Circle the words you don't know.

Nouns	**Verbs**	**Adjectives**	
chemicals	to take a nap	alert	complex
	to wake up	deprived	enough

2. Guess the meanings of the underlined words. Write your guess on the lines. Check your answers with a dictionary or your teacher.

1. Many people worry about the <u>chemicals</u> in food. They think some chemicals might cause cancer or other diseases.

   My guess: _____

2. A baby needs to sleep a lot. Most babies <u>take a nap</u> every morning and afternoon.

   My guess: _____

3. It's hard <u>to wake up</u> in the morning. I have a loud alarm clock to wake me up.

   My guess: _____

4. In Norway, the days are very short in the winter. People are <u>deprived</u> of sunshine. They are very happy when spring comes.

   My guess: _____

5. A simple math problem is 2 + 6 = 8. A <u>complex</u> problem is
   $x = [y^2 * 324y - (x + 2y)]$

   My guess: _____

6. I ate two pieces of cake. That was <u>enough</u> cake. I don't want any more.

   My guess: _____

7. There is a lot of traffic on this road. Before you walk across it, look carefully to the left and to the right and listen for cars coming quickly. You have to be <u>alert</u> on this road.

   My guess: _____

Listen

3 **Listening for Main Ideas.** Listen to the conversation. As you listen, answer these questions.

1. What's wrong with Ali?
2. Is Beth worried about Ali?
3. What is this conversation about?

4 **Listening for Specific Information.** Listen again. Circle the letter of the best answer to each question.

1. What did Ali do last night?
   a. He went to the library.
   b. He went to a party.
   c. He ate food with chemicals.

2. What happens when you study but don't sleep?
   a. You forget the information you studied.
   b. You have more time to study.
   c. It's OK if you eat the right foods.
3. Beth says that eating foods like fish helps you _____.
   a. sleep
   b. forget
   c. study

After You Listen

5   **Vocabulary Review.**   Complete these sentences. Use words from the list.

to wake up	chemical	to take a nap
(to feel / be) deprived (of)	(to be) alert	enough

1. Do you want to go to the movies? I have _____ money for two tickets.
2. My grandfather gets sleepy every afternoon, so he likes _____ for about an hour.
3. I have a test early tomorrow. Please_____ me _____ in time for class.
4. Caffeine is the _____ in coffee that keeps you awake.
5. Away from home, I felt _____ of my family and their love.
6. Drivers should always be _____. Careless driving causes accidents.

Stress

6   **Listening for Stressed Words.**   Listen to the first part of the conversation again.

1. The stressed words are missing. Fill in the blanks with words from the list.

bed	late	OK	slept	up
before	matter	party	study (two times)	Why
friend	meet	partying	test (two times)	

Beth: Ali! What's the __*matter*__ ? Can't you wake _____ this morning?
                            1   2

Ali: I was up _____ last night. My _____ had a _____.
                        3   4   5

          I only _____ about 4 hours.
                         6

Alicia: _____ didn't you stay in _____ this morning?
                    7   8

Ali: I have to _____ my _____ group at the library. We have a big
            ₉   ₁₀

_____ next week.
   ₁₁

Beth: A big _____? Why didn't you _____ last night instead of
                     ₁₂   ₁₃

_____?
   ₁₄

Ali: Oh, it's _____ I studied a lot _____ the party.
                      ₁₅   ₁₆

2. Now read the conversation with a partner. Practice stressing words correctly.

Pronunciation

Numbers

Numbers can be difficult to understand. Some numbers in English sound very much the same. The difference between the "teens" and the "tens" is mostly stress: the ending "-teen" is stressed more than the ending "-ty." Also, "-ty" is often pronounced "-dy."

Examples:	**teens**	**tens**
	13- thir-teen'	30- thir'-dy
	14- four-teen'	40- four'-dy
	15- fif-teen'	50- fif'-dy
	16- six-teen'	60- six'-dy
	17- seven-teen'	70- seven'-dy
	18- eight-teen'	80- eight'- dy

7 **Pronouncing Teens and Tens.**   Listen and repeat these examples of "teens" and "tens."

Teen	**Ten**
1. He is <u>fourteen</u> years old.	He is <u>forty</u> years old.
2. I bought <u>thirteen</u> new books.	I bought <u>thirty</u> new books.
3. The price is <u>seventeen</u> dollars.	The price is <u>seventy</u> dollars.
4. It happened in <u>1918</u>.	It happened in <u>1980</u>.
5. We stayed for <u>fifteen</u> days.	We stayed for <u>fifty</u> days.
6. I live at <u>16</u> New Hope Road.	I live at <u>60</u> New Hope Road.

8 **Distinguishing between Teens and Tens.** Listen to the sentences. Circle the letter of the sentence that you hear.

1. a. He is <u>fourteen</u> years old.	b. He is <u>forty</u> years old.
2. a. I bought <u>thirteen</u> new books.	b. I bought <u>thirty</u> new books.
3. a. The price is <u>seventeen</u> dollars.	b. The price is <u>seventy</u> dollars.
4. a. It happened in <u>1918</u>.	b. It happened in <u>1980</u>.
5. a. We stayed for <u>fifteen</u> days.	b. We stayed for <u>fifty</u> days.
6. a. I live at <u>16</u> New Hope Road.	b. I live at <u>60</u> New Hope Road.

Talk It Over

1. Work in groups of four. Write the names of your group members in the spaces at the top of the chart.
2. Look at the example (Stacy). Practice asking your teacher the questions and write his / her answers on the chart.

   Example: Do you go to bed early or late?

                       I go to bed late.

3. Then ask your group members the questions. Write their answers on the chart.

Questions	Stacy	Teacher	Name	Name	Name
1. Do you go to bed early or late?	I go to bed late				
2. Do you get up early or late?	I get up late				
3. What do you do when you can't sleep?	I read				
4. Are you a "morning person" or a "night person"?	A night person				
5. What language do you dream in?	English				
6. What kind of dreams do you enjoy the most?	Dreams about adventures				
7. Do you ever have nightmares (bad dreams)?	Sometimes				
8. Do you believe dreams can tell the future?	Yes				
9. Your question:					

4. Write down your dreams for a week. Then share your dreams with your group.

PART 2	# Listening Skills

Getting Meaning from Context

1   Using Context Clues.

1. Listen to this discussion about sleep. It is in five parts. Listen to the beginning of each part.
2. Listen to the question. Circle the letter of the best answer.
3. Then listen to the last part of the conversation to hear the best correct answer.

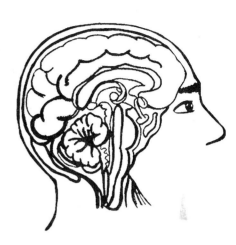

1. What are you listening to?
   a. conversation
   b. telephone call
   c. lecture in a classroom

2. What does sleep do for your brain?
   a. nothing
   b. keeps your brain healthy
   c. makes you forget things

3. Why did Carlyle Smith teach the students a list of words and a difficult problem?
   a. to see if they could do the problem
   b. to teach them English
   c. to see how much they remembered

4. Why did Smith have the students sleep different amounts on the first, second, and third nights?
   a. to see if sleeping after learning helps memory
   b. to see if the students became angry
   c. to make the students sick

5. How did the students who didn't sleep much on the first or third nights remember the difficult problem?
   a. the same as the other students
   b. they remembered better than the students who got enough sleep
   c. they didn't remember the difficult problem well

Listening to a Lecture

Before You Listen

2   **Preparing to Listen.**   Before you listen, discuss these questions with a partner.

1. When you listen to a lecture, do you take notes? What information do you try to write down?
2. Do you review your notes before taking a test?
3. Do you try to sleep well before a test or do you stay up late studying?

3   **Vocabulary Preview.**   Listen. Circle the words and expressions you don't know.

Nouns	**Adjectives**	**Verb**
subject group	sleep-deprived	to solve
percent	complex	

Listen

4   **Listening for Main Ideas.**   You are going to listen to some results from the research on sleeping. As you listen, mark the following statements as True or False.

_____   The subjects in this research study were all students.

_____   Being sleep-deprived affected all the subjects the same way.

_____   The subject groups all had the same test scores.

5   **Listening for Test Scores.**   Listen again. Fill in the information in the table below.

	Percent correct on the test	
Subject group	**List of words**	**Complex problem**
Enough sleep all nights		100%
Sleep-deprived first night	100%	
Sleep-deprived second night		
Sleep-deprived third night		70%

After You Listen

6   **Discussing the Lecture.**   Work with a partner.

1. Look at the sentences about the research. Decide if they are True or False. Report to the class. Does everyone agree?

    1. _____   The test on the matching pairs of words showed no differences between the groups of students.

2. _____ Students who slept enough every night answered all the questions correctly.

3. _____ Students who were sleep-deprived the first night forgot 30% of the matching pairs.

4. _____ Students who were sleep-deprived the first night forgot 30% of the complex problem.

5. _____ Students who slept enough the first night but not the second night forgot 30% of the complex problem.

6. _____ Students who slept the first night and the second night, but not the third night forgot 30% of the complex problem.

7. _____ The study shows that sleeping enough does not affect your memory.

2. How much sleep is enough? Find out how many hours each student in your class usually sleeps. Write the numbers below. Then report the results in percentages. For example,

> 10 students in the class
> 3 usually sleep 7 hours at night.
> You say: "30% of the students sleep 7 hours a night."

	# of Students	Percentages
5 hours	_____	_____
6 hours	_____	_____
7 hours	_____	_____
8 hours	_____	_____
9 hours	_____	_____
10 hours	_____	_____

Listening to a Dream

Before You Listen

7 **Preparing to Listen.** Before you listen, talk about dreams with a partner.

1. Do you remember your dreams?

2. Do you dream in color or black and white?

3. Do you usually have pleasant dreams or unpleasant ones?

4. Why do you think people dream when they sleep?

8   **Vocabulary Preview.**   Listen to these words and phrases. Match the words and phrases with the correct picture.

1. diving flippers or fins
2. snorkel tube
3. face mask
4. bathing trunks or bathing suit

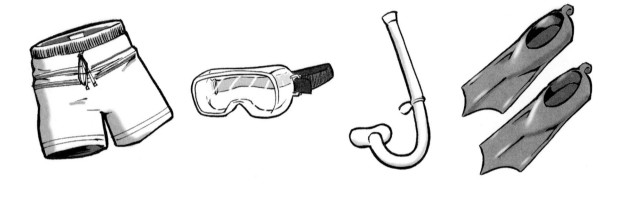

_____   _____   _____   _____

Listen

9   **Listening for Main Ideas.**   Now listen to the information. As you listen, think about what happens in Ali's dream. Circle the picture below that shows what happens.

Picture 1   Picture 2

10 **Listening to a Dream.** Listen again. Look at the pictures below. Number each picture in the order of the story.

—————

—————

—————

—————

After You Listen

11 **Discussing a Dream.** Discuss these questions with a partner.

1. Where did Ali go with Beth in his dream?

   _____

2. Why was everyone on the bus looking at Ali?

   _____

3. Why did Beth have to pay for the tickets?

   _____

4. What was the surprise at the end of the dream?

   _____

12 **Retelling a Dream.**   Now retell the dream by filling in the blanks.

1. Ali dreamed that he was going _____.

2. When Ali arrived at Beth's house, he was wearing _____

    _____.

3. Beth told Ali to _____.

4. Ali couldn't do what Beth wanted because he couldn't _____.

5. Then, Ali and Beth took a _____ to go to the movies.

6. Everyone on the bus looked _____.

7. When they got to the movie theater, Ali couldn't move his arms so Beth

    _____.

8. Inside the theater, everyone was wearing _____.

9. Beth felt very _____.

PART 3

Reading

Before You Read

1   Can you answer the following questions? Compare your answers in small groups.

1. Why do we sleep?
2. Does everyone dream?
3. What do dreams mean?

You Try It!

Put a piece of paper and a pen or pencil next to your bed. When you wake up after a dream, write down as much as you can remember about it. You will need this information for Part 4.

2 **Vocabulary Preview.** Let's review some ways to understand the meaning of a word without using a dictionary. Write answers in the blanks.

Sometimes the meaning of a new word follows the word.

1. He says his theory is correct, but a theory is only an idea or a guess.

   A theory is _____ *an idea or a guess.* _____

The meaning of a word sometimes is in parentheses.

2. Our bodies produce a growth hormone (a chemical that helps us grow).

   A growth hormone is _____

Sometimes we can use our basic knowledge of the subject to guess the meaning.

3. Scientists believe that birds evolved from dinosaurs.

   Evolved means _____

The meaning of a word often follows a dash (—):

4. The light turned on and off randomly—without any pattern or meaning.

   Randomly means_____

Sometimes a writer uses two words that mean almost the same thing. If you know one word, you can guess the other.

5. We need sleep to repair and fix our bodies.

   Repair means something like _____

Other times we can use the context—the sentences that follow the word.

6. There was a lot of evidence that George killed Mr. Smith. Police found George's gun in Mr. Smith's house. Also, two people saw George leaving Mr. Smith's house. In addition, everyone knew that George hated Mr. Smith.

   Evidence is _____

7. He was interested in Chinese culture. He studied Chinese art, history, language, and religion.

   Some examples of *culture* are_____

8. He wasted money all the time. He spent it on expensive meals, he bought new clothes he didn't need, and he drove an expensive car he couldn't afford.

   Waste means _____

Are the following terms opposite or similar? Write O (for *opposite*) or S (for *similar*) on the line.

_____O_____ 1.   activity — sleep

_____ 2.   theory — idea

_____ 3.   save — waste

_____ 4.   lazy — active

_____ 5.   disease — medical problem

_____ 6.   megalopolis — city

_____ 7.   company — business

Read

3   Read the article. Try to understand the meanings of new words without using a dictionary.

Sleep and Dreams

A | No one really knows why we sleep. There are two theories, but a theory is only an idea or a guess—scientists don't know if these theories are correct or not.

B | One theory of sleep is called the "Repair Theory." This theory says that during the day we use many important chemicals in our bodies and brains. We need sleep to make new chemicals and repair and fix our bodies. One piece of evidence for this theory is that our bodies produce more of a growth hormone (a chemical that helps us grow) while we sleep.

C | Another theory is called the "Adaptive Theory." This theory says that sleep evolved because it stopped early humans and animals from wasting energy and putting themselves in danger from the other animals that killed and ate them; in other words, sleep kept them safe and out of trouble. It was necessary for their survival.

D | Whatever the reason for sleep, everyone sleeps and everyone dreams every night. Many times we don't remember our dreams, but we still dream. Like sleep, no one knows exactly why we dream or what dreams mean. There have been many theories about dreams throughout history. Many cultures believe that dreams can predict the future—that they can tell us what is going to happen to us. Sigmund Freud and other psychologists and psychiatrists believe that dreams can tell us about our feelings and desires.

E | However, some scientists now believe that dreams mean nothing at all—dreams are caused by the electrical activity in our brains while we sleep. These scientists believe that nerve cells fire randomly and our brains try to make a story out of these meaningless patterns. These scientists say that dreams seem crazy and without meaning sometimes because they are crazy and without any meaning at all.

After You Read

4 Read the article again. Every paragraph has a letter. What is the main idea of each paragraph? Write the paragraph letters on the lines.

_____E_____ Dreams may not mean anything.

_____ There are many theories about what dreams mean.

_____ Sleep may help our bodies prepare for a new day.

_____ Scientists have two theories about why we sleep.

_____ It is possible that sleep protected us from dangers.

Discussing the Reading

5 Talk about your answers to the following questions with a partner or in small groups.

1. Do you remember your dreams? What do you think dreams mean?
2. Does your family or culture have special meanings for some kinds of dreams? Do these dreams tell about the future?
3. Do you believe one of the two theories about why we sleep? Why or why not?

PART 4

Writing

Using Sentence Patterns

Sentence Pattern 7. Some verbs are not like transitive or intransitive verbs. They are more like the verb be — they can connect a subject with an adjective or a noun. These verbs are called *linking* verbs.

subject	+	linking verb	+	adjective or noun
George		felt		happy.
George		seemed		sad.
George		became		a teacher.

Linking verbs include

verbs of perception

The house	smelled	strange.
The music	sounded	beautiful.
The girl	looked	pretty.

Many adjectives that follow linking verbs describe positive or negative feelings. Look at the adjectives in the following box. Put them in the Positive or Negative column. (If necessary, use a dictionary to look up the meanings of the adjectives.)

nervous	anxious	wonderful	healthy	happy	sad	comfortable	uncomfortable
great	depressed	lost	strange	terrible	terrific	worried	relaxed	confident

Positive

wonderful

_____

_____

_____

_____

_____

_____

_____

Negative

nervous

_____

_____

_____

_____

_____

_____

_____

Now list five adjectives to describe the feelings in your dream.

_____ _____ _____ _____ _____

Practicing the Writing Process

1   **Exploring Ideas: Free Writing.**   Write for ten minutes about one of your dreams. Include as many details as you can. Now tell a partner about your dream. Use your freewrite, but don't read it aloud. While you listen to your partner's dream, think about the following two questions:

1.   Can you understand the dream? What is it about?
2.   Are there interesting details?

Ask your partner questions about his or her dream.

2   **Writing the First Draft.**   Write a first draft of a narrative of your dream. Remember to include the actions, your feelings and what you saw, heard, smelled, tasted, and felt.

3   **Editing.**   Read the student's dream narrative that follows. The student made five errors with the past tense. Correct the errors.

> I dreaming I was in Paris. The city was beautiful and I feeled happy. I could see the Eiffel Tower. I can smell flowers because it was spring. I walkd along a street. A man asks me for directions.

Now check your first draft for errors. Use the following checklist.

Editing Checklist

1. Does every subject have a verb?
2. Are your past tense verb forms correct?
3. Do your sentences begin with capital letters?
4. Do other words in the writing need capital letters?
5. Do your sentences end with periods or other final punctuation?

4   **Peer Editing.**   Show your narrative to another student. Read each others paragraphs and discuss each other's work.

5   **Writing the Second Draft.**   Write your second draft and give it to your teacher.

Writing a Journal

6   Write a journal entry about something that happened to you. Use the past continuous tense to set the scene. Use adverbs, phrases, and clauses to make the time clear.

> It was very late at night. I was walking home from a party. I opened the door of my apartment. Before I turned on the light, I heard a shriek and I jumped! It was my cat. I stepped on its tail.

PART 5   # Grammar

A. Simple Past Tense: Irregular Verbs

Simple Form	Past Tense Form	Notes
become	became	Some verbs do not use -ed
begin	began	in the past form. These are
come	came	called irregular verbs. Here
do	did	are nine irregular verbs.
eat	ate	There are many others. For
freeze	froze	a more complete list see
go	went	pages 000–000.
have	had	
put	put	

1   Use the past tense to complete these sentences.

1. Johnny's dreams _____*were*_____ (be) always the same. He _____ (have) wings

                  1   2

   like a bird. He _____ (be) in the air all of the time; he _____ (not be) on

                           3   4

   the ground at all. He _____ (not go) very high above the ground, but he

                                     5

   _____ (go) fast and far. He _____ (not eat) worms and berries. He _____

  6   7   8

   (eat) hamburgers and french fries. He always enjoyed those dreams.

2. For a long time my dreams _____ (be) frustrating. Sometimes I _____

                                            9   10

   (go) to the post office in my college. I _____ (begin) to turn the lock. I

                                                   11

   _____(not do) it right. I could never open it! Other times, I _____ (be) at

  12   13

   a public telephone. I _____ (become) frustrated because I _____ (not have)

                                   14   15

   the correct number. Have you ever had a dream like that?

3. My math teacher _____ (have) a funny dream. Her dream _____ (begin)
     ₁₆   ₁₇

    in our English class. She _____ (come) into the usual room, but the students
                                        ₁₈

    _____ (not be) the usual students. All of the students _____ (be) famous
        ₁₉   ₂₀

    people. The Backstreet boys _____ (not have) their homework. Enrique Iglesias
                                       ₂₁

    _____ (eat) a hamburger and fries quickly and then _____ (begin) to sing
       ₂₂   ₂₃

    the answers to the exercise. What a strange dream!

B. Using *Too* with Short Statements

Long Form	Short Form	Notes
Marcella had a dream about ice cream, and Mario had a dream about ice cream. John sees color in his dreams, and Susan sees color in her dreams.	Marcella had a dream about ice cream and Mario **did too**. John sees color in his dreams, and Susan **does too**.	When *and* joins two affirmative statements. *too* is sometimes used to make the second statement shorter. The second statement usually has an auxiliary (not a main) verb.

Note: You can use other auxiliaries and helping verbs with *too*: John sees color in his dreams, and Susan **does** too. I can answer the question, and you **can** too.

C. Using *Either* with Short Statements

Long Form	Short Form	Notes
Marcella didn't eat fish in her dreams, and Mario didn't eat fish in his dreams. They won't be late, and we won't be late.	Marcella didn't eat fish in her dreams and Mario **didn't either**. They won't be late, and we **won't either**.	When *and* joins two negative statements, use *either* instead of *too*. The second statement usually has an auxiliary (not a main) verb.

Note: You can use other auxiliaries and helping verbs with *either*: I'm not tired of grammar, and she **isn't** either. They won't be late, and we **won't** either.

2   Sigmund Freud and Carl Jung were psychoanalysts who believed that dreams could explain emotions. Look at the chart here. Then make sentences with *too* and *either*.

Sigmund Freud

Sigmund Freud (1856–1939) was the originator of psychoanalysis for the treatment of psychological problems.

Carl Jung

Carl Jung (1875–1961) was a Swiss psychiatrist. His theories about using dreams to understand people have influenced many psychiatrists around the world.

		Sigmund Freud	**Carl Jung**
1.	was born in the 1800's	Yes	Yes
2.	lived in Europe	Yes	Yes
3.	studied in the United States	No	No
4.	interpreted dreams	Yes	Yes
5.	worked primarily with children	No	No
6.	had many children	No	No
7.	was a professor at Harvard University	No	No
8.	could speak German	Yes	Yes
9.	had an interest in mental illness	Yes	Yes
10.	studied acupuncture in China	No	No
11.	died in the United States	No	No
12.	is still important in the field of psychiatry	Yes	Yes

Example:

Freud was born in the 1800s and Jung was too.

3   **Talking About Dreams.**

- Together, plan the story of a dream and the interpretation of it.
- Then practice a role-play of your dream / analysis session. One person is the analyst and the other is the patient.
- Perform your role-play for the class.

Example: Doctor, last night I had a very bizarre dream. I was a microchip in Bill Gates's laptop computer....

D. Simple Past Tense: More Irregular Verbs

Simple Form	Past Tense Form	Simple Form	Past Tense Form
bring	brought	know	knew
find	found	leave	left
get	got	speak	spoke
grow	grew	take	took
grow up	grew up	understand	understood

4   Use the past tense of the verbs in parentheses to complete these sentences.

1. Mika _____ (not grow up) in the United States.

2. She _____ (grow up) in Japan.

3. Mika _____ (have) many strange dreams the first month after she came to the U.S.

4. One night, she _____ (find) herself under the sea.

5. She _____ (not find) any other people there.

6. She _____ (not get) scared.

7. In fact, she _____ (get) accustomed to her new surroundings.

8. She _____ (speak) to an orange octopus and a pink sea horse.

9. Unfortunately, they _____ (not speak) Japanese or English.

10. Then she _____ (leave) them to look for someone familiar.

11. But, the octopus _____ (not leave) her side.

12. As a result, she _____ (bring) him with her.

13. She _____ (not bring) the sea horse.

14. Somehow she _____ (know) the octopus was an old friend.

15. She _____ (not know) where to go next.

16. She _____ (take) a turn at a big rock.

17. Then she _____ (understand) the true identity of the octopus.

E. *Used to*

Examples	Meanings	Notes
You **used to sleep** 17 to 18 hours a day. You **used to wear** diapers when you were a baby.	(You don't sleep 17 to 18 hours a day now.) (You don't wear diapers now.)	*Used to* is followed by a simple verb. It means that something was true in the past but isn't true anymore.

5 Your life is different now from when you were a baby. Read each statement below about when Charlie was a baby. Then tell what is true for Charlie now.

Example: Charlie used to sleep 15 hours a day.
Now he sleeps only 6 hours a night.

1. Charlie used to crawl on the floor.

2. Charlie used to eat with his fingers.

3. Charlie used to cry when he was hungry.

4. Charlie used to drink milk from a bottle.

5. Charlie used to sit in a high chair.

6. Charlie used to sleep in a crib.

7. Charlie used to play with toys all day.

8. Charlie used to sleep with a teddy bear.

6 Think about when you were 13 years old. Sit in a circle. Tell one thing you *used to* do when you were 13 years old. Explain if you still do this or if you don't do it anymore.

F. Simple Past Tense: More Irregular Verbs

Simple Form	Past Tense Form	Simple Form	Past Tense Form
hear	heard	give	gave
know	knew	lend	lent
say	said	see	saw
think	thought	make	made

7 Complete these sentences. Use the past forms of the verbs in parentheses.

1. I _____heard_____ (hear) that many people had sleep problems.

2. I _____ (not hear) that doctors had all of the answers.

3. Sam _____ (not know) that he snored.

4. His wife _____ (know) that he had a serious problem.

5. His wife _____ (say), "You need to see a doctor."

6. The doctor_____ (not say) his problem was funny.

7. We _____ (not think) his problem was serious.

8. The doctor _____ (think) Sam had sleep apnea.

9. Joan's sister _____ (give) her a book called <u>The Joy of Flying!</u>

10. She _____ (not give) her a book about airplane crashes.

11. Tom _____ (not lend) her ear plugs.

12. Her friend _____ (lend) her a sleep mask.

13. On TV Joan _____ (see) a commercial for a special travel store.

14. She _____ (not see) a commercial for pet food.

15. Sue _____ (make) a list of all of the reasons to enjoy flying.

16. She _____ (not make) a list of reasons to avoid flying.

8 Complete the reading with the past tense forms of the verbs in parentheses.

My grandmother always _____said_____ (say), "I _____ (never have) a good
          1   2

night's sleep after I _____ (marry) your grandfather. The reason _____
                      3   4

(be) that my grandfather snored. "For months I _____ (put) a pillow over my
                                                 5

head when I _____ (go) to bed. That _____ (be) not a good solution, and
             6   7

it _____ (not work)." Next she _____ (buy) earplugs, but she _____
   8   9   10

(not like) to sleep with them. She _____ (hear) about an herbal tea, so she
                                    11

_____ (make) it for my grandfather every night for a month. Unfortunately, that
   12

_____ (not help) either. At that time, doctors _____ (not think) that
   13   14

snoring _____ (be) a problem. Too bad for Grandpa! Too bad for Grandma!
        15

9 **Writing a Story.**   Finish the following story. Use the verbs in this chapter and others.
Write at least three more sentences. Read your stories in your group. Choose one story
to read to the whole class.

My brother Jim had a big problem. He couldn't get up in the morning.

Video Activities: Children and Sleep

Before You Watch.

1. How long do most people need to sleep every night?
    a.   6 hours   b.   8 hours   c.   10 hours   d.   12 hours

2. What does our "internal clock" tell us?

    a.   when to eat
    b.   the time of day
    c.   when to sleep and wake up

Watch.

1. How long do young children need to sleep every night?
    a.   6 hours   b.   8 hours   c.   10 hours   d.   12 hours

2. What happens to children who are "sleep-deprived" (who don't get enough sleep)? Check all that apply.

    _____ They don't want to get up in the morning.
    _____ They work harder.
    _____ They can't concentrate very well.
    _____ They get into trouble at school

Watch Again.

1. Check the things that make children stay up later according to the video.
    _____ homework   _____ television   _____ internal clock
    _____ computers   _____ lights   _____ parents

2. How quickly can you change a child's internal clock?
    a.   one hour a week
    b.   two hours a day
    c.   one hour a day
    d.   three hours a week

After You Watch.   Combine the following sentences with *too, either* or *even though*.

1. My daughter didn't sleep well last night. My son didn't sleep well last night.

2. They went to bed early. They couldn't fall asleep.

3. I read them a story. My husband read them a story.

4. My daughter wasn't tired. My son wasn't tired.

5. This morning my daughter didn't want to get up. This morning my son didn't want to get up.

6. They had school. I let them sleep late.

Chapter 7

Work and Lifestyles

| PART 1 | # Listening to Conversations |

Before You Listen

1   **Preparing to Listen.**

Look at these photos.

Computer programmers in shared cubicle

Architect looking at plans

Which of these jobs would you like to have? Why?

2   **Vocabulary Preview.**   Ali and Alicia are at the Faber College Career Planning and Placement Center. They are at the job announcement board looking for summer jobs.

1.   Listen to these words from their conversation. Circle the ones you don't know.

Nouns	Adjectives	Verbs
public health	part-time	look for
reporter	full-time	find out
journalism		
experience		

2.   Guess the meanings of the underlined words. Write your guess on the lines. Check your answers with a dictionary or your teacher.

1.   Lee worked last summer for a computer software company. He got a lot of good <u>experience</u> in programming and designing video games.

My guess: _____

2.   There are many ways to <u>find out</u> what jobs are available. You can read the paper, look on the Web, call local companies, or ask people you know.

My guess: _____

3. Thousands of people in my city became sick with the flu last year. This was a <u>public health</u> problem, so the government and the doctors worked together to solve the problem.

   My guess: _____

4. Beth is unhappy with her current job. She is <u>looking for</u> a job where she can work with children.

   My guess: _____

5. After the plane crash, the <u>reporter</u> had to interview the families of the passengers, then write a story about them for the newspaper.

   My guess: _____

6. Ali is still in school, so he doesn't have time for a <u>full-time</u> job. He wants a <u>part-time</u> job for about 20 hours a week.

   My guess: _____

7. Alicia is studying <u>journalism</u>. Does she want to work for a newspaper or a TV news show?

   My guess: _____

Listen

3 **Listening for the Main Idea.**

Listen to the conversation and answer this question.

What are Alicia and Ali doing?

4 **Listening for Specific Information.** Listen again and answer these questions.

1. What kind of job does Ali want?
2. Where did Ali work last summer?
3. Where did Alicia work last summer?
4. What kind of news stories does Alicia want to write someday?
5. How did Alicia find her job last summer?

After You Listen

5 **Discussing Main Ideas.** Work with a partner. Discuss the answers to these questions.

1. What are some ways that Ali and Alicia are using to find jobs?
2. Why does Alicia think Ali should look for a job on the Web?
3. Why do you think Alicia and Ali want jobs related to their majors?

6 **Vocabulary Review.** Complete these sentences. Use words from the list.

public health	part-time	look for
reporter	journalism	find out
experience	full-time	

1. Alicia wants to get more _____ in journalism so she can get a good job after graduating.
2. A _____ might write local news stories or international news stories.
3. Students often take _____ jobs while they are in school to earn money or get experience in their majors.
4. Alicia thinks that the Web is a good way to _____ _____ a job because you can find jobs all over the world.
5. The Website for the Centers for Disease Control and Prevention at www.cdc.gov has a lot of good information on _____ _____ problems such as malaria, tuberculosis, and flu epidemics.
6. A career in _____ often means that you have to travel a lot to get information for your news stories.
7. If you want to _____ _____ more about jobs in journalism, you should talk to someone at your local newspaper.

Stress

7 **Listening for Stressed Words.** Listen to the first part of the conversation again.

1. The stressed words are missing. Fill in the blanks with words from the list. Some words may be used more than once.

do	hoping	major	reporter
Egypt	isn't	newspaper	summer job
experience	journalism	part-time	sure
great	looking for	public health	writing

Alicia: What are you _____ , Ali?
₁

Ali: I'm _____ to find a _____ in my
₂   ₃

_____ , _____ .
₄   ₅

Alicia: I'm _____ you can, Ali. Do you have any _____
₆   ₇

Ali: Yes, I _____ . I worked _____ in a lab in
₈   ₉

_____ last summer.
₁₀

Alicia: That's _____ . I want to find a job _____
₁₁   ₁₂

for a local _____ . I'd like to be a _____ .
₁₃   ₁₄

Ali: Your major's _____ , _____ it?
₁₅   ₁₆

2. Now read the conversation with a partner. Practice stressing words correctly.

Pronunciation: Majors versus Job Titles

Someone who majors in *accounting* from a university will become an *accountant*. The difference in pronunciation is small, but important. Usually, the last unstressed syllable shows the difference.

8 **Pronouncing Majors and Job Titles.** Listen and repeat the following examples of majors and job titles.

Major	Job Title
accounting	accountant
psychology	psychologist
biology	biologist
journalism	journalist
physics	physicist
technology	technologist
economics	economist

9 **Distinguishing between Majors and Job Titles.** Listen to the sentences. Circle the letter of the word that you hear.

1. a. journalism
   b. journalist
2. a. economics
   b. economist
3. a. psychology
   b. psychologist
4. a. accounting
   b. accountant
5. a. biology
   b. biologist
6. a. physics
   b. physicist
7. a. technology
   b. technologist

Talk It Over

What's the best job for you? Work with a partner. Ask your partner the questions below. Write your partner's answer (yes or no) in the space.

_____ 1. Do you enjoy sitting at a computer for a long time working or playing games?

_____ 2. Do you like to work with other people to complete a task or plan a project?

_____ 3. Do you enjoy writing reports for school or work?

_____ 4. Are you good at working with details, such as numerical figures?

_____ 5. Do you like to solve problems by finding new ways of looking at them?

_____ 6. Do you like to plan your own schedule and decide when you are going to work?

_____ 7. Do you enjoy using your hands to build something?

_____ 8. Do you like discussing problems with others to make a decision?

_____ 9. Do you want a profession where you can help other people?

_____ 10. Do you like to be in charge—to tell other people what to do?

_____ 11. Do you think you work best by myself?

_____ 12. Are you happy doing the same things every day so you know what to expect?

_____ 13. Do you like the challenge of learning to do new things frequently?

_____ 14. Do you like to meet new people?

_____ 15. Do you expect to work 12–14 hours a day?

_____ 16. Are you happy when you know exactly what's expected of you?

_____ 17. Are you good at persuading people to do what you want?

_____ 18. Do you want to feel secure in your job?

_____ 19. Do you like to travel?

Now look at the jobs below. What job do you think is the best for your partner? Why? Tell the class why you think this is the best job for your partner.

a. programmer
b. civil engineer
c. medical doctor
d. sales representative
e. teacher
f. accountant

g. bank teller
h. secretary
i. restaurant manager
j. travel writer for a magazine
k. computer graphics designer
l. hotel manager

Listening Skills

Getting Meaning from Context

1 **Vocabulary Preview.** Listen to these words and expressions from the conversations. Circle the ones that you don't know.

Noun	Verb	Adjectives
appointment	get out of	tired of
		rough

2 **Using Context Clues.**

1. Listen to the first part of each conversation.
2. Listen to the question and circle the letter of the best answer.
3. Then listen to the last part to hear the correct answer.

1. Who is Alicia talking to?
    a. an English teacher
    b. a reporter
    c. a job interviewer for a newspaper

2. What does Lee want to do this summer?
    a. work in a hospital
    b. study
    c. go back to Korea

3. What is David thinking about doing this summer?
    a. studying
    b. going to Europe
    c. visiting his friend in San Francisco

4. What does David want to do in the fall?
    a. work
    b. travel
    c. study

5. Can Lee work?
    a. No, he can't.
    b. Yes, but only in the summer.
    c. Yes, but he has to finish school first.

Listening to Job Interviews

Before You Listen

3 **Preparing to Listen.**   Before you listen, talk about job interviews with a partner.

1.   Have you ever had an interview for a job?
2.   What do you think an employer wants to know about a job applicant?

4 **Vocabulary Preview.**   Listen to these words and expressions. Circle the ones you don't know.

Nouns	**Adjectives**
resumé	challenging
	accurate
	impressive

Listen

5 **Listening for Main Ideas.**   Rafael is interviewing for a job. He's talking to Mrs. Kline. As you listen to the interview, answer these questions.

1.   Why is Rafael interested in the job?
2.   What job would Rafael like to have in ten years?

6 **Listening to Job Interviews.**   Listen again. This time, circle the answers to the questions.

1.   Why should Mrs. Kline give Rafael a job with the company?
    a.   He learns quickly.
    b.   He needs the money.
    c.   He thinks the job sounds easy.

2.   Why does Rafael need to learn things quickly?
    a.   He doesn't know anything about computers.
    b.   He has to go back to school if he takes the job.
    c.   He'll have to learn a lot of new things if he takes the job.

3.   What would Rafael like to do in ten years?
    a.   be a department store clerk
    b.   be a manager
    c.   be a student

After You Listen

7 **Discussing Job Interviews.**   How would you answer the following common job interview questions? Think about what the interviewer wants to know. Discuss your answers in small groups.

1.   What are your strengths?
2.   What are your weaknesses?
3.   What is your biggest accomplishment?
4.   Why do you want this job?

Listening to Future Plans

Before You Listen

8 **Preparing to Listen.**   In small groups, talk about planning for the future.

1.   What are some situations where people ask you about your plans for the future?
2.   Who do you talk to about your plans for the future? Your family? Your friends? Your teachers?

9 **Vocabulary Preview.**   Listen to these words and expressions. Circle the ones you don't know.

Nouns	**Expression**
relatives	once in a lifetime
youth hostels	
construction	
expenses	

Listen

10 **Listening for the Main Idea.**

David is talking to his father about going to Europe this summer with his friend, Bill. As you listen to their conversation, try to answer this question.

What does David want his father to do?

11   **Listening to Future Plans.**   Listen again. As you listen, choose the best answer to each question.

1.   What did David do last summer?
   a.   traveled in Europe
   b.   worked for a construction company
   c.   stayed in youth hostels

2.   What does David have to pay for this summer?
   a.   a rental car, hotel rooms, and meals
   b.   airfare, hotel rooms, and meals
   c.   airfare and meals

3.   How will David pay for the trip?
   a.   money saved from his part-time job
   b.   borrow from his friend Bill
   c.   money from selling his car

4.   What does David need from his father?
   a.   money for his books and expenses
   b.   French lessons
   c.   a new car

5.   Which of these is NOT a reason that David thinks the trip is a good idea?
   a.   he can learn about the world
   b.   he can earn some money
   c.   he can practice his French

After You Listen

12   **Discussing the Conversation.**   In small groups, discuss your answers to the following questions.

1.   Do you think David's father will let him go to Europe with his friend?

2.   What are some concerns David's father might have about David's plans?

3.   Can you think of any other reasons David could give his father?

4.   Do you think traveling is good preparation for your career? Why or why not?

PART 3	**Reading**

Before You Read

1 Look at the photos and answer the questions with a partner or a group.

1. Who are these people?
2. What are they doing? Why?

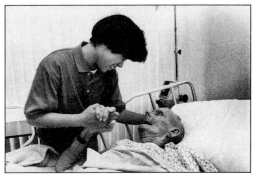

Photo 2

Photo 1

Photo 3

2 **Vocabulary Preview.** Sometimes a colon (:) can help you understand a new word. If you know the key word or words on one side of the colon, then you can figure out the meaning of the word or words on the other side of the colon.

Examples: There are terrible diseases: AIDS, cancer, and TB.

What are some examples of diseases? _AIDS, cancer, and TB_

She cooked some wonderful foods: stews, casseroles, and soufflés.

What are stews, casseroles, and soufflés? _some wonderful foods_

Look at the words before and after the colon in each sentence. Then answer the questions.

1. They look around their neighborhoods and see terrible hardships: sickness, loneliness, and homelessness.

   What are some terrible hardships? _____

2. He started a group, TreePeople, to plant trees: pine, elm, cypress, and eucalyptus.

   What are pine, elm, cypress, and eucalyptus? _____

3. Volunteers help sick ocean mammals: seals, sea lions, and sea otters.

   What are seals, sea lions, and sea otters? _____

Read

3   Read the article.

Volunteers

A | Some people go to work each day and then come home. They spend time with their family and friends. Maybe they watch TV or go to a movie. Sometimes they exercise or read. This is their life. But for other people, this isn't enough. They look around their neighborhoods and see people with terrible hardships: sickness, loneliness, and homelessness. Other people see problems with the environment. Many people want to help. They volunteer. They give some of their time to help others.

B | Volunteers help in many ways. Some visit sick and lonely people. Some give their friendship to children without parents. Some build houses for homeless people. Others sit and hold babies with AIDS.

C | Andy Lipkis was at summer camp when he planted his first tree. He began to think about the environment. In many countries, people were cutting down trees. Andy Lipkis worried about this. In 1974, he started a group, TreePeople, to plant trees: pine, elm, cypress, and eucalyptus. Today there are thousands of members of TreePeople, and more join every day. They plant millions of trees everywhere.

D | Ruth Brinker wasn't planning to change the world. Then a young friend became sick. He had AIDS. Soon he was very sick, and he couldn't take care of himself. Brinker and other friends began to help him. In 1985, Brinker started Project Open Hand. This group cooks meals and takes them to people with AIDS. Soon Project Open Hand volunteers were cooking 1,100 meals every day. This number is growing. Ruth Brinker didn't plan to change the world, but she is making a change in people's lives.

E | At the Marine Mammal Center in northern California, volunteers help sick ocean mammals: seals, sea lions, and sea otters. The sick animals become well and strong. Motherless baby animals grow big and healthy. For many weeks—or sometimes months—volunteers help to feed and take care of these ocean animals. They don't get any pay for their hard work. Their "pay" is the good feeling on the day when a healthy animal can return to its home—the ocean.

F   Twenty or thirty years ago, most volunteers were housewives. They volunteered time while their husbands were working. Today both men and women volunteer. There are volunteers from all social classes, all neighborhoods, and all ages. Most aren't rich or famous. They enjoy their volunteer work. People need them. Today, with problems such as AIDS and homelessness, the world needs volunteers more than ever before.

After You Read

4   **Finding the Main Ideas.**   Read the story again. Every paragraph has a letter. What is the main idea of each paragraph? Write the letters on the lines.

_____D_____ One woman started a group to take meals to people with AIDS.

_____ Some people give time each week to help others.

_____ Volunteers help in different ways.

_____ Different kinds of people are volunteers.

_____ One man started a group to plant trees.

_____ Some people help sick ocean animals.

5   **Making Good Guesses.**   Circle the correct letter to complete the sentence.

The writer thinks _____.

a.   volunteers are unhappy people

b.   people are afraid of AIDS

c.   volunteers do important work

Discussing the Reading

6   In a small group, answer and discuss the following questions.

1.   What kinds of volunteers are in your country?

2.   Do you volunteer? If so, what do you do? Where do you volunteer?

3.   What volunteer work is interesting to you?

PART 4

Writing

Using Past Tense Verbs

Fill in the missing simple past form of each of the following verbs.

1. write _____

2. volunteer _____

3. talk _____

4. cook _____

5. sit _____

6. become _____

7. meet _____

8. get _____

9. tell _____

10. ask _____

11. keep _____

12. decide _____

13. start _____

14. know _____

15. answer _____

16. seem _____

Sometimes we are asked to write about a job experience—either as part of an English writing test or for a job application. A good writer always thinks about the person who will read his or her writing—the writer's "audience." For example, if you are writing about your work skills and experience, you want to make a good impression on your audience. Read the following job experience narrative. Like many students, the writer had a problem. She was only 20 years old and had no formal job experience because she had always been a student. But notice that she found an important job to write about anyhow.

    The most important job I ever had was taking care of my little sister. From the time I was five or six, I took care of her. Both my parents worked, and I was like a mother to her. I had to dress her and feed her, watch over her, and keep her out of danger. This was a lot of responsibility for a young girl, and there were times when I just wanted to go out and play and forget about my sister. But I knew I couldn't do this.

    My job was difficult, but I learned some important things. First, I learned responsibility. I always do my schoolwork now because I learned to be responsible. Also, I learned how difficult it is to raise a child. I plan to wait until I finish college before I get married and have a child.

What verb tenses did the writer use and why? Compare your answers with a partner's.

Practicing the Writing Process

1 **Exploring Ideas: Free Writing.**   You are going to write about one of your work experiences. To get some general ideas down on paper, complete the following sentences. Don't worry about spelling or correct grammar.

1.   My most important work experience was _____
     _____

2.   At this job, I _____
     _____

3.   From this job, I learned _____
     _____

Now think of some details about your work experience that will make your narrative interesting. For example, think of specific information. Write down these details in the spaces after the following questions. Again, don't worry about spelling, grammar, or punctuation.

What exactly did you do on this job?
_____

_____

How did the job make you feel?
_____

_____

What difficulties were there?
_____

_____

What did the workplace look like?
_____

_____

What were the people you worked with like?
_____

_____

What did you like most about the job?
_____

_____

2 **Writing the First Draft.**   Write your first draft of your job experience narrative.

3 Editing.   Most of the verbs in your narrative should be in the simple past tense. Check your verbs. Are they in the simple past? Are they regular or irregular? Is the form correct?

Now edit your first draft. Use the following checklist to correct any mistakes.

Editing Checklist

1. Are your past tense verb forms correct?

2. Does every subject have a verb?

3. Do your sentences begin with capital letters?

4. Do other words in the writing need capital letters?

5. Do your sentences end with periods or other final punctuation?

4 Peer Editing.   Show your narrative to another student. Read and discuss each other's work. Are any of your job experiences the same?

5 Writing the Second Draft.   Now write your second draft and give it to your teacher.

Writing a Journal

6 Write a journal entry about a time you helped someone with a task. For example, helping a younger brother or sister assemble a toy, helping a relative in a business, or helping around the house. Use the simple past tense verbs in Part 4 if you can.

After my uncle's house was flooded, I helped him clean the first floor. We moved the furniture outside. We dried the floors with mops and rags. We cleaned the walls.

PART 5 | Grammar

A. Past Continuous Tense: Affirmative Statements

Examples	Notes
I **was working**. He / she / it **was working**. You / we / they **were working**.	Use the past continuous tense to talk about past activities in progress at specific times such as *a minute ago, yesterday, last week, last month*, or *last year*.

1 What was the man in the pictures doing five years ago? What is he doing now? Read this story and find out.

Then and Now

Five years ago, Andre Cardoso was living in an apartment with his aunt and uncle in Chicago, Illinois. His parents were sending him money. He was studying English and taking computer classes. He liked his English classes, but he loved his computer classes. He was learning as much as possible as fast as possible. At the same time he   5 was meeting new people and making new friends. Life was great!

After just one year, Andre got a job with a small company in Chicago. He was very good at his job. Eight months later, he got a better job. In the next three years, Andre changed jobs four more times!

Now Andre is living in his own apartment in San Francisco, Cali-   10 fornia. He is still working with computers. In fact, he has his own company—Cardoso Consulting. He is very busy, but very happy. He is making a lot of money and he loves his work. Life looks beautiful for him.

---

2 Underline all the past continuous verbs in the reading.

3 Meet Andre's neighbors. Complete these sentences. Use the past continuous tense of the verbs in parentheses.

1. Hi. I'm Ana. I used to be a teacher, but I wanted to be an actress. Last year I

   _____ (live) in Hollywood. I _____ (try) to get a job in the
         1   2

   movies. I _____ (dream) about my first movie. Now I'm a waitress. But
                          3

   you know what? I like it!

2. Hello. My name is Fred. I always wanted my son to go to college, and he did go.

   After college, my son _____ (work) with computers, and he
                                    1

   _____ (invent) lots of crazy things. Big companies _____
         2   3

   (call) him. They _____ (try) to buy some of his inventions. I
                          4

   _____ (take) the phone messages. Now he's working in a car wash.
         5

   What happened?

B. Past Continuous Tense: Negative Statements

Long Form	Contraction
I / she / he / it **was not working**.	I / she / he / it **wasn't working**.
You / we / they **were not working**.	You / we / they **weren't working**.

4 Carolina is Andre's sister. Complete her story with the past continuous tense of the verbs in parentheses.

Hi. I'm Carolina, Andre's younger sister. While Andre _____ in Chicago, I
                                                                 1

_____ (study) Hotel Management in New York. I _____ (not live)
         2   3

in the dormitory. I _____(stay) with my cousins in Connecticut. I
                            4

_____ (not work) because I _____ (spend) two hours a day on
         5   6

the train. My cousins _____ (not speak) any English to me, and I
                                 7

_____ (not learn) very fast. I _____(not feel) happy or
         8   9

successful. I _____ (get) a little depressed and frustrated. I didn't know
                      10

what to do to change my situation.

C. Past Continuous Tense: Yes / No Questions and Short Answers

Yes / No Questions	Short Answers	
	Affirmative	**Negative**
Was I **working**?	Yes, I **was**. Yes, you **were**.	No, I **wasn't**. No, you **weren't**.
Was she / he / it **working**?	Yes, she / he / it **was**.	No, she / he / it **wasn't**.
Were you / we / they **working**?	Yes, you / they / we **were**.	No, you / they / we **weren't**.

5 Write the questions for these statements.

1. _Were you living here last month?_ _____

   Yes, I was living here last month.

2. _____

   No, Carolina wasn't living in the dormitory.

3. _____

   No, Carolina wasn't working.

4. _____

Yes, Carolina was spending a lot of time on the train.

5. _____

No, her cousins weren't speaking English with her.

6. _____

Yes, I was studying hard last night.

7. _____

No, I wasn't speaking my native language in English class!

8. _____

No, our teacher wasn't speaking to us in Russian.

D. Past Continuous Tense: Information Questions

Questions	Possible Answers
What was he **doing** yesterday?	He was working.
Where were we **meeting** last year?	We were meeting in San Francisco.
When was it **arriving**?	It was arriving at 3:00.
Why were you **taking** a course last month?	Because I wanted to.
How was she **doing**?	She was doing well.
How much was he **earning**?	He was earning a lot of money.

Questions	Possible Answers
Who was doing that job?	John was doing it.
Who was calling all last night?	David was.

6   Use these question words to complete the sentences below. More than one word can be used in some sentences.

Who   What   When   Where   Why   How   How much

1. _____ were you doing at 10:00 last night?

2. _____ was helping you with the assignment?

3. _____ was he going?

4. _____ were you getting to work?

5. _____ was he running out the door?

6. _____ were you earning last year?

7 **Information Gap.** Here is more information about Andre and Carolina. One partner is Student A. Look only at the chart labeled Student A. The other partner is Student B. Look only at the cart labeled Student B. Ask information questions to complete your chart.

Student A				
Name	10 years ago / living	Last year / dating	Last year / earning	Now earning
Andre	_____	Mina	_____	$200,000 a year
Carolina	Brazil	_____	$2,000 a month	_____

Student B				
Name	10 years ago / living	Last year / dating	Last year / earning	Now earning
Andre	Brazil	_____	$40,000 a year	_____
Carolina	_____	nobody	_____	nothing

E. The Past Continuous Versus the Simple Past

Examples	Notes
Kyong Ah **got up** every day at 6:00.	Use the simple past tense for past repeated action.
Kyong Ah **went** to bed at 10:00.	Use the simple past tense for a short action at a specific time in the past.
Kyong Ah **was sleeping** at 11:00.	Use the past continuous tense for an action in progress in the past.

8 Circle the correct verbs in these sentences.

Example: Andre ((ate) / was eating) breakfast quickly at 6:00 every morning.

1. Andre (went / was going) to bed at 1:00AM in Brazil.
2. Andre (slept / was sleeping) at 6:00 in the morning.
3. Andre (worked / was working) seven days a week in San Francisco.
4. Carolina (worked / was working) at 9:00 last night.
5. Carolina (served / was serving) dinner when the lights went out.
6. The customers (ate / were eating) by candlelight while the manager was calling an electrician.
7. Kyong Ah (traveled / was traveling) to Europe last summer.
8. The students (studied / were studying) four hours every day.

F. The Past Continuous Versus the Simple Past with *While*

Use while with the past continuous tense to show the longer action. Use the simple past tense for the action that interrupts or stops the longer action. Use a comma only when while is at the beginning of the sentence.

While + past continuous tense + simple past tense	Simple past tense + *while* + past continuous tense
While Carolina **was working**, she **met** an interesting young man.	Carolina **met** an interesting young man **while** she **was working**.
While she was **picking up** an order, he **asked** her for a date.	He **asked** her for a date **while** she **was picking up** an order.

9 Complete each sentence with the simple past tense or the past continuous tense of the verb in parentheses.

Example: While Andre was working in Chicago, he _____*decided*_____ (decide) to start his own business.

1. While Andre was planning his new business, he _____ (realize) San Francisco would be a perfect location.

2. While Andre was moving to San Francisco, he _____ (start) to feel nervous.

3. After one week in his new office he was beginning to think that he had made a mistake. While he was worrying, he _____ (receive) a phone call. It _____ (be) his first customer!

4. While he _____ (talk) to the customer, his pen ran out of ink.

5. While he was looking for another pen, the phone call _____ (be) disconnected.

6. Another customer came through the door while Andre _____ (try) to call the man back.

7. While he was talking to the new customer, the phone _____ (ring).

8. Another customer came into the office while he _____ (answer) the phone.

9. While Andre _____ (introduce) himself to the latest customer, he received a fax.

10. Two hours later, while he _____ (have) lunch, Andre decided that he needed an assistant.

Video Activities: Dentist Fashion Designer

Before You Watch.

1. Match the careers in Column A with the descriptions in Column B.

A	**B**
1. fashion designer	a. takes pictures
2. dentist	b. paints pictures
3. photographer	c. makes clothes
4. artist	d. fixes teeth

2. Which of the careers above is different from the others? Why?

Watch.   Circle the correct answers.

1. Steve Schneider is a _____.
    a. dentist   b. photographer   c. fashion designer

2. Steve Schneider _____.

    a. likes dentistry as much as fashion design
    b. doesn't like having two careers
    c. started designing clothes in college

Watch Again.

1. Steve Schneider has designed clothes for _____.

    ___ Arnold Schwarzennegger
    ___ Bruce Springsteen
    ___ Tom Cruise
    ___ Sharon Stone

2. Put a D next to the benefit of being a dentist. Put an F next to the
    benefit of being a fashion designer.

    ___ make more money
    ___ talk to people
    ___ work alone

After You Watch.   Discuss these questions in small groups. What are the
three most important things in choosing a career? Why?

a. making a lot of money
b. having a high social status
c. working with people
d. having the opportunity to travel
e. staying near my family

Chapter 8

Food and Nutrition

PART 1	# Listening to Conversations

Before You Listen

1   **Preparing to Listen.**   Look at this photo.

1.   Where are these people?
2.   Do you ever eat in restaurants like this? Why or why not?

2   **Vocabulary Preview.**   David, his girlfriend Meryl, and Ali's friend Pat are waiting in line at a popular restaurant.

1.   Listen to these words from their conversation. Circle the ones you don't know.

Nouns		**Adjectives**
order of	calories	good / bad for you
picnic	vegetarian	worried about
diet		

2.   Guess the meanings of the underlined words. Write your guess on the lines. Check your answers with a dictionary or your teacher.

1.   Let's make some sandwiches, go to the park, and have a <u>picnic</u>.
My guess: _____

2.   Meryl eats a lot of salads, so Pat is not <u>worried about</u> Meryl's health.
My guess: _____

3.   *Waiter:* What would you like?
Customer: I'd like a cheeseburger and an <u>order of</u> fries.
My guess: _____

4.   He's sick because he smokes, and smoking is <u>bad for you</u>.
My guess: _____

5. Pat doesn't eat hamburgers. She's a <u>vegetarian</u>.
    My guess: _____

6. Meryl doesn't like sugar in her food, so she will have a <u>diet</u> cola.
    My guess: _____

7. Cheeseburgers have a lot of <u>calories</u> because they have a lot of fat.
    My guess: _____

Listen

3 **Listening for the Main Idea.**   Listen to the conversation. As you listen, answer this question.
    Where are David, Meryl, and Pat?

4 **Listening for Specific Information.**   Listen again. This time, answer these questions.
    1. What is David going to order?
    2. What is bad about cheeseburgers?
    3. What is bad about sugar?
    4. What is good about salad?

After You Listen

5 **Discussing Main Ideas.**   Work with a partner. Discuss the answers to these questions.
    1. What foods do Meryl and Pat think are bad for you?
    2. What foods do they think are good for you?
    3. Do you agree with Meryl and Pat?

6 **Vocabulary Review.**   Complete these sentences. Use words from the list.

calories	worried about	picnic
diet	order of	bad for you

1. Foods with a lot of sugar, like soft drinks, usually have a lot of _____ in them.
2. Meryl and Pat are _____ _____ David's health because he eats too many hamburgers.
3. Do you think _____ foods really help you lose weight?
4. We can take a long walk and eat a _____ lunch on the way.
5. Doctors think that foods with a lot of fat, like red meat and ice cream, are _____ _____ _____.
6. With my tofu, I'd like a side _____ _____ rice, please.

Stress

7   **Listening for Stressed Words.**   Listen to the first part of the conversation again.

1.   The stressed words are missing. Fill in the blanks with words from the list.

cheeseburger	fries	hungry	picnic
eat	have	like	what
fat	healthy	order	worried

Meryl: What are you going to _____, David?

1

David: I'm _____! I want a double _____ and a

2   3

large _____ of _____.

4   5

Pat: Ugh! How many cheeseburgers do you _____ every week?

6

You had a couple at the _____ yesterday, didn't you?

7

David: Yeah, . . . so _____? I _____ cheeseburgers!

8   9

Meryl: I think Pat's _____ about you.

10

David: Why? I'm _____.

11

Pat: But cheeseburgers have a lot of _____.

12

2.   Now read the conversation with a partner. Practice stressing words correctly.

Reductions

8   **Comparing Long and Reduced Forms.**   Listen to the following sentences. They contain reduced forms. Repeat them after the speaker.

Long Form	**Reduced Form**
1. What are you going to have?	What're ya gonna have?
2. I think I'm going to have some tofu and rice.	I think I'm gonna have some tofu and rice.
3. We would like a couple of salads.	We'd like a coupla salads.
4. Isn't there a lot of fat in cheeseburgers?	Isn't there a lotta fat in cheeseburgers?
5. They don't want to eat lots of fatty food.	They don't wanna eat lotsa fatty foods

9 **Listening for Reductions.** Listen and circle the letter of each sentence you hear. If you hear a reduction*, circle the letter of the reduced sentence, even though it is not a correct written form.

1. a. What are you going to have?
   b. What're ya* gonna* have?
2. a. I think I am going to have some tofu and rice.
   b. I think I'm gonna* have some tofu and rice.
3. a. We would like a couple of salads.
   b. We'd like a coupla* salads.
4. a. Isn't there a lot of fat in cheeseburgers?
   b. Isn't there a lotta* fat in cheeseburgers?
5. a. They don't want to eat lots of fatty food.
   b. They don't wanna* eat lotsa* fatty food.

Talk It Over

With a partner, talk about the twelve items below. Are they good or bad for you? Why? Discuss your decisions with the class.

Example: french fries

      A: Are french fries good for you?
      B: No I don't think so.
      A: Why not?
      B: Because they have a lot of fat.

1. soda
2. cigarettes
3. orange juice
4. cheeseburgers
5. beer
6. rice
7. tofu
8. vegetables
9. beans
10. ice cream
11. skim (nonfat) milk
12. salad dressing

Listening Skills

Getting Meaning from Context

1 **Vocabulary Preview.** You are going to hear some conversations about food. Listen to these words and expressions from the conversations. Circle the ones you don't know.

Nouns	Verb
charge	to beat
teaspoon	
onion soup	
carrot	
cucumber	
produce	
ounce	

2 **Using Context Clues.**

1. Listen to the first part of each conversation.
2. Listen to the question and circle the letter of the best answer.
3. Then listen to the last part to hear the correct answer.

1. Where are Lee and Alicia?
   a. in a restaurant   b. in a supermarket   c. in a cafeteria

2. What's Lee asking about?
   a. the waiter   b. the menu   c. the bill

3. What are David and Beth doing?
   a. cooking something
   b. shopping
   c. eating in a restaurant

4. Where are Ali and Alicia?
   a. at a restaurant
   b. at a produce stand (a small fruit and vegetable market)
   c. in a supermarket produce (fruit and vegetable) section

5. Which spaghetti sauce is the best buy?
   a. the spaghetti sauce with mushrooms
   b. the eight-ounce size for $1.06
   c. the size for 99 cents

Listening to Instructions

Before You Listen

3 **Preparing to Listen.**   Talk with a partner. When do you give someone instructions? List some possible situations. Share with the class.

4 **Vocabulary Preview.**   Listen to these words and expressions from the conversation. Circle the ones you don't know.

Noun	**Verbs**	**Adverb**
cheese grater	to chop	thoroughly
	to grate	
	to brown	

Listen

5 **Listening for Main Ideas.**   Beth and Alicia are talking to Ali. As you listen to their conversation, try to answer these questions.

1. What kind of instructions did Ali's mother send him?
2. Why did Ali ask his mother for recipes?

6 **Listening to Instructions.**   Listen again.

1. This time, match the words on the left with the meanings on the right.

_____ 1. chop   a. a tool for making thin pieces of cheese

_____ 2. mix   b. cook something in oil until it changes color

_____ 3. grate   c. cut something into small pieces

_____ 4. brown   d. combine two or more things together

_____ 5. cheese grater e. make thin, little pieces of cheese or other foods

2. Listen again. Check your answers. Then compare with a partner.

After You Listen

7 **Discussing Food.**   If you want to learn new recipes, you need to know the names of many different food items. How many do you know in English?

1. Work in groups of five. Each member of the group chooses one letter of the alphabet. Write one letter in each of the five boxes across the top of the following chart. You are going to write a word in each space that fits the category and starts with the letter at the top of the column.

    For example, if the category is *Fruits* and the letter at the top of the column is A, you can write *apple* in the space. Fill in as many spaces as you can in three minutes.

2. When you finish, take turns reading your answers in your group. Cross off any answers that another member in the group says. You get one point for each answer you wrote that no one else has. The person with the most points wins.

Category					
Fruits					
Vegetables					
Grains					
Meats					
Desserts					
Drinks					

Following Recipes

Before You Listen

8   **Preparing to Listen.**   Before you listen, talk about cooking and recipes with a partner.

1. Do you like to cook? Why or why not?
2. What is something you can cook? Describe it.
3. Describe any TV shows about cooking that you have seen.

9 **Vocabulary Preview.**   Match these food words with the pictures.

a.

b.

c.

d.

e.

f.

g.

1. _____ beef

2. _____ beans

3. _____ tomatoes

4. _____ onion

5. _____ oil

6. _____ chili powder

7. _____ shredded cheese

Listen

10 **Listening for the Main Idea.**   Wally Chan has a cooking show on TV. He explains how to make easy American dishes. As you listen to Wally Chan's show, answer this question.

What food is Wally making?

11   **Ordering Steps in a Recipe.**   Look at these pictures. They show the steps for making chili, but the steps are in the wrong order. Listen to Wally's show again and number the pictures from 1 to 4.

———   ———   ———   ———

After You Listen

12   **Discussing Opinions about Food.**

1.   Now listen to the following statements. Decide if you agree or not. Write True or False for each of the statements.

———   1.   I like onions on my hamburgers.

———   2.   Chili powder makes food too hot and spicy.

———   3.   I eat a lot of cheese—with crackers, bread, and on other foods.

———   4.   Tomatoes are best in salad, with lettuce, oil, and vinegar.

———   5.   I like beans when they are cooked with onions and garlic.

———   6.   Cooking with oil can make you fat.

———   7.   The best pizza has just tomato sauce and lots of cheese.

———   8.   Foods like beans, rice, and potatoes should be eaten at every meal.

———   9.   Onions are good cooked and uncooked.

———   10.   I like a lot of pepper in my food.

2.   Compare your answers with the class.

| PART 3 | **Reading** |

Before You Read

1 Look at the photos. Discuss the questions with a partner or in small groups.

1. How are these two photos different?
2. In your opinion, what was important to the people in the first photo? What's important to the people in the second photo?

Photo 1

Photo 2

2 **Vocabulary Preview.** Sometimes you can understand a new word if you know its opposite. *Big* is the opposite of *small*. *Terrible* is the opposite of *wonderful*. If you know one of these words, you may not need a dictionary for the other.

Example: The people in the first picture aren't <u>slender</u>; they're overweight.
The opposite of *slender* is <u>overweight</u>.

On the blanks, write the opposites of the underlined words.

1. People thought, "How <u>attractive</u>!"—not "How ugly!"
   The opposite of *attractive* is _____.

2. Many of the vegetables are <u>raw</u>. They aren't cooked because cooking takes away some vitamins.
   The opposite of *raw* is _____.

3. They want to be <u>slim</u>, not fat.
   The opposite of *slim* is _____.

4. Sometimes people lose weight fast, but they usually <u>gain</u> it again.
   The opposite of *gain* is _____.

Match the meanings with the underlined words. Write letters on the lines.

_____ 1. pictures

_____ 2. not fat or heavy at all

_____ 3. what you eat

_____ 4. foods from milk and cream

_____ 5. a sickness

_____ 6. people who paint pictures

a. The dancer was light and <u>slender</u>.

b. Leonardo Da Vinci and Picasso are two famous <u>artists</u>.

c. Many people die from <u>heart disease</u> every year.

d. The <u>paintings</u> were on the wall of the museum.

e. The butter and cheese are in the <u>dairy</u> section.

f. His <u>diet</u> had too much meat and too few vegetables.

Read

3   Read the article. As you read, think about the main ideas of the article.

New Foods, New Diets

A   On March 26, 1662, Samuel Pepys and four friends had lunch at his home in London, England. They ate beef, cheese, two kinds of fish, and six chickens. They didn't eat any fruits or vegetables. More than three hundred years ago, people in Europe ate differently from today. They looked different too. In famous paintings by Titian, Rubens, and other artists, people weren't slender; they were overweight. But people three hundred years ago thought, "How attractive!"—not "How ugly!"

B   Today people are learning more about health. People in North America and Europe are changing their way of eating. They're eating a lot of fruits and vegetables. Many of the vegetables are raw. They aren't cooked because cooking takes away some vitamins, such as vitamins A, B, and C. People are eating less sugar. They're not eating much red meat. They're drinking less cola and coffee. They're eating low-fat foods.

C   People these days want to be slender, not fat. Sometimes people in North America go a little crazy to lose pounds. Thousands of them join diet groups, go to special diet doctors, or spend a lot of money at diet centers. Each year Americans spend more than $30 billion on diets and diet products. Sometimes people lose weight fast, but they usually gain it back again. Almost 95 percent of all people gain back weight after a diet.

D   Diets are changing in many countries, but this isn't always good news. For example, the Japanese diet was very healthful for many years. People ate a lot of fish and vegetables. Now they're eating more and more beef, sugar, and dairy products—ice cream and cheese. This seems similar to Samuel Pepys's party, doesn't it? The problem with this change in diet is easy to see. There is more sickness such as heart disease. The changing diet is not good for the health of the Japanese people.

E   Sometimes people go crazy over food. They eat lots of bad foods because they taste good. Or, other times, they do the opposite—eat very little because they want to be slender. When will people learn? Too much food, too little food, and the wrong foods are all bad ideas.

After You Read

4 **Finding the Main Ideas.** Circle the number of the main idea of "New Foods, New Diets."

1. It's important to eat fruits and vegetables.
2. People today eat differently from people in the past.
3. People in the past were fat; people today are not fat.
4. The way of eating today is better than in the past.

5 Read "New Foods, New Diets" again. Every paragraph has a letter. What is the main idea of each paragraph? Write the letters on the lines.

_____E_____ People sometimes go crazy over food.

_____ Europeans in the past ate differently from today, and they were overweight.

_____ The Japanese way of eating is changing, but the change isn't good.

_____ The way of eating in Europe and North America is changing.

_____ Today Americans don't want to be overweight. They do many things to lose weight.

6 **Making Good Guesses.** Circle the correct letter to complete the sentence.

The author (writer) of "New Foods, New Diets" probably _____.

a. doesn't like crazy diets
b. eats a lot of meat, sugar, and dairy products
c. is a member of a diet group

Discussing the Reading

7 Talk about your answers to the following questions with a partner.

1. How much meat do you eat? How often do you eat fruits and vegetables?
2. What do people eat in your community? Fill in the chart.

	United States in General		Your Community
Breakfast	cereal juice coffee fruit	or	ham eggs toast coffee	
Lunch	sandwich salad milk	or	soup salad bread	
Dinner	chicken green vegetables potato fruit ice cream			

PART 4   # Writing

Using the Command Form of Verbs

Here are a student's directions about how to do something. It is a recipe. Before you read it, find out what these words mean—*swirl, stir, flip*. Ask your teacher, other students, or look in your dictionary.

How to Stir-Fry Chicken

The ingredients are chicken (cut into small pieces), chopped garlic, and ginger.

First heat a wok (a Chinese frying pan) or other frying pan until hot. Next add 2 tablespoons of oil and swirl the oil around to cover the surface of the pan. Heat until hot. Then turn the heat to medium, put in the ginger and garlic, and stir a few times. Now turn the heat to high and put in the chicken, stirring it quickly around in the pan. Keep turning it and flipping it with a spatula for about one minute or until it is white. Finally, add the seasoning sauce. (The seasoning sauce is 2 tablespoons of soy sauce mixed with a tablespoon of sugar and four tablespoons of Chinese rice wine.)

When we write about how to do something (describe a process), we often use what is called the "command form" of the verb. It is the simple or infinitive form of the verb. The subject of this verb—*you*—is not stated. We give commands (directions) with only the verb.

(subject)	+	**verb**	
(*you*—not stated)		Turn	the heat to medium.

Underline all the command forms in the recipe "How to Stir-Fry Chicken." Then check your answers with a partner.

Also, when we describe a process, we usually use sequence words such as *first, second, third*, etc., or *next, now, then*, and *finally* to indicate or signal the steps in the process. Underline all the sequence words in the recipe. What kind of word comes immediately after them? Share your answers with a partner.

Practicing the Writing Process

1 **Exploring Ideas: Free Writing.** You are going to write directions about how to do something. Write about anything, such as preparing a special food, washing a car, making a dress, or fixing a broken window. Write for ten minutes about how to do it—the basic steps. Don't worry about spelling, grammar, or punctuation.

2 **Writing the First Draft.** Write your first draft. Begin by reviewing your freewrite. Make sure all the steps are there and in the correct sequence.

3 **Peer Editing.** Now check your work. Use the following list to help correct any mistakes. Then share and discuss your work with a partner.

Editing Checklist

1. Are the verb forms correct—are most of them in the simple (command) form?

2. Are there sequence words to signal the steps?

3. Do your sentences begin with capital letters?

4. Do other words in the writing need capital letters?

5. Do your sentences end with periods or other final punctuation?

---

4 **Writing the Second Draft.** Write your second draft and hand it in to your teacher.

PART 5

Grammar

A. Count Nouns

A noun names a person, place, thing, idea, or emotion. There are two basic types of nouns—count nouns and noncount nouns. Count nouns are things you can count, such as chairs and people. Noncount nouns are things you can't count, such as water and air.

To make the plural form of most count nouns, add -s to the noun. Some nouns have spelling changes in the plural, and a few nouns have irregular plurals.

Count Nouns with Spelling Changes		
Singular	**Plural**	**Notes**
box	boxes	For nouns ending in the letters *s, sh, ch, x,* and
city	cities	*z,* add -*es* to the noun.
potato	potatoes	
shelf	shelves	For nouns ending in a consonant + *y,* change
Irregular nouns:		the *y* to *i* and then add -*es.*
child	children	
man	men	Some nouns ending in *o* add -*es.*
foot	feet	

1   Write the plurals of these regular and irregular count nouns.

1. person _people_   5. radio _____   9. loaf _____
2. party _____   6. goose _____   10. dish _____
3. child _____   7. church _____   11. tomato _____
4. orange _____   8. mouse _____   12. woman _____

B. *Some* and *Any* with Count Nouns

	Examples	Notes
Question	Do you have **any** apples at home? Would you like **some** apples?	Use *some* or *any* in questions.
Affirmative statement	I have **some** apples at home.	Use *some* in affirmative statements.
Negative statement	I don't have **any** oranges at home.	Use *any* in negative statements.

2   Imagine that you are Mark or Linda. Look at the picture of "your" kitchen, but not at your partner's picture. Ask questions about your partner's kitchen, using *any*.

Examples:

apples
A: Linda, do you have any apples?

B: Yes, I have some.

potato chips
B: Mark, do you have any potato chips?
A: No, I don't have any.

1. grapes   4. carrots   7. canned tomatoes
2. peas   5. onions   8. frozen dinners
3. oranges   6. bananas   9. potatoes

C. Noncount Nouns

Noncount nouns can be ideas (*freedom*), feelings (*love*), activities (*golf*), or things we measure (*oil*) or group together (*furniture*). Noncount nouns are always singular. Do not add -*s* to these nouns, and do not use *a* or *an* with them.

Noncount Nouns			Count Nouns		
Examples		**Notes**	**Singular**	**Plural**	**Notes**
bread butter coffee	flour rice tea	People usually measure these items.	apple banana potato	apples bananas potatoes	People usually count these items.

3 Write *C* in front of count nouns and *N* in front of noncount nouns.

1. _C_ apple
2. ____ tomato
3. ____ rice
4. ____ cheese

5. ____ banana
6. ____ meat
7. ____ egg
8. ____ juice

9. ____ milk
10. ____ potato
11. ____ sugar
12. ____ sandwich

D. *Some* and *Any* with Noncount Nouns

	Examples	**Notes**
Question	Would you like **some** tea? Do you have **any** coffee at home?	Use *some* or *any* in questions.
Affirmative statement	I have **some** Columbian coffee at home.	Use *some* in affirmative statements.
Negative statement	I don't have **any** tea at home.	Use *any* in negative statements.

4 Choose a shopping list. Ask each other questions about the lists using *some* or *any*. Write down your partner's answers, but do not look at your partner's list.

Student A

> Shopping List
> ice cream
> lettuce
> mustard
> ketchup
> milk
> rice
> coffee
> meat

Student B

> Shopping List
> butter
> tea
> jam
> cheese
> sugar
> milk
> coffee
> bread
> cereal

Examples: butter
A: *Do you need some butter?*
B: *Yes, I do.*

butter
B: *Do you need any butter?*
A: *No, I don't.*

1. rice
2. milk
3. coffee
4. sugar

5. tea
6. mustard
7. jam
8. ketchup

9. cereal
10. meat
11. ice cream
12. lettuce

E. Common Counting Units

Counting units are used with many kinds of food and household items. *Of* follows all these expressions except *dozen*. In measurement and recipes, other units are also used, such as *yards* and *teaspoons*.

Unit	Examples
bag	flour, potatoes, potato chips, sugar, etc.
bar	candy, hand soap, etc.
bottle	detergent, ketchup, juice, soda, and other liquids
box	cereal, laundry detergent, etc.
bunch	bananas, carrots, grapes, green onions, flowers, etc.
can	soda, soup, vegetables, tuna, etc.
carton	eggs, ice cream, milk, etc.
dozen	eggs
gallon, quart, pint	all liquids, ice cream, yogurt
head	cabbage, cauliflower, lettuce
jar	jam, mayonnaise, mustard, peanut butter, etc.
loaf	bread
package	cookies, potato chips, spaghetti, etc.
piece	bread, cake, meat, cheese, etc.
pound, ounce	cheese, meat, poultry, fruits, vegetables, etc.
roll	paper towels, toilet paper, etc.
tube	toothpaste, hand cream, etc.

5 Write the correct counting unit under the picture of each type of food below. Some foods can have more than one counting unit.

| of sugar | of soda | of soup | of milk | eggs |

| of lettuce | of pickles | of bread | of cheese | of cheese |

F. Questions with *How much* and *How Many*

Questions	Possible Answers	Notes
How much bread should I buy?	Buy two loaves of bread, please.	Use *how much* in questions with noncount nouns.
How many bananas do you have? **How many** eggs do you need for the cake?	I have three. I don't need any.	Use *how many* in questions with count nouns.

6 Use a questionnaire to find out what people in your class or community eat. Ask three different people questions with *how much* or *how many*. Add two questions of your own. Then work in small groups and compare your answers.

How much or how many?	Name _____	Name _____	Name _____
1. cups of coffee or tea / drink / every day			
2. rice / eat / each week			
3. salads / eat / in a month			
4. sandwiches / eat / in a week			
5. water / drink / when you exercise			
6. times a week / eat / in fast-food restaurants			
7. pieces of cake / have / for dessert			
8. bread / have / with dinner			
9.			
10.			

Video Activities: Diets

Before You Watch.

1. People on diets usually want to _____.
    a. lose weight   b.   gain weight   c.   get stronger

2. Check the foods that people on restrictive diets usually cannot eat.
    _____ ice cream   _____ fruit   _____ candy   _____ butter
    _____ vegetables   _____ chicken   _____ bread   _____ rice

Watch.

> **Vocabulary Note**
> A crash diet is very restrictive. People on crash diets are usually trying to lose weight very quickly.

1. Dr. Goodrick explains why restrictive diets are _____.
    a. good for you   b.   dangerous   c.   necessary for some people

2. Check all of the things that Dr. Goodrick says a crash diet can do.
    _____ change your brain chemistry
    _____ help you stay thin
    _____ make you want to eat more
    _____ make you gain weight

Watch Again.

1. How long should it take to get used to a low-fat diet?
    a. almost 6 weeks   b.   at least 6 months   c.   about 6 days

2. Check all of the things that you should do to lose weight.
    _____ eat only fruits and vegetables
    _____ change your eating habits slowly
    _____ eat fewer than 1,200 calories a day
    _____ find friends to help you
    _____ try new ways of cooking
    _____ stop eating high-fat foods immediately
    _____ plan your meals
    _____ exercise

After You Watch.   Complete the following conversation with *a little, a few, a lot(of), much,* or *many*.

A. I know I'm not fat but I'd like to lose _____ weight.

B: How _____ weight do you want to lose?

A: Just _____ kilos, maybe five or six. I'm trying not to eat _____ fat or sugar. That's difficult for me because I usually eat _____ cookies.

B: How _____ cookies do you eat in one day?

A: Maybe three or four.

B: How _____ exercise do you do?

A: _____. I run ten kilometers a day

Chapter 9

Great Destinations

| PART 1 | # Listening to Conversations |

Before You Listen

1 **Preparing to Listen.**   In small groups, talk about places you have visited.

1. What places have you visited?
2. What places in the world would you like to visit?
3. Do you prefer to fly, drive, or take the train when you travel?

2 **Vocabulary Preview.**   It is spring break. David, Beth, and Ali are in Kyoto, Japan for the Cherry Blossom festival.

1. Listen to these words and expressions from their conversation. Circle the ones you don't know.

Nouns	Verbs	Adjective
scenery	to pull over	rugged
flat tire	to change (a tire)	
spare tire		
blossoms		

2. Guess the meanings of the underlined words. Write your guess on the lines. Check your answers with a dictionary or your teacher.

1. Japan is a beautiful country with a lot of wonderful <u>scenery</u>: mountains, lakes, beaches, and towns.
    My guess: _____

2. A car has five tires: four on the wheels and one called a <u>spare tire</u>.
    My guess: _____

3. My car has a <u>flat tire</u>. I think there's a hole in it.
    My guess: _____

4. I'm going to <u>pull over</u> to the side of the road and stop the car.
    My guess: _____

5. I had <u>to change</u> the flat tire. Now I need to buy a new tire to replace the spare.
    My guess: _____

6. Visitors to Japan enjoy the beautiful <u>blossoms</u> on the cherry trees in the spring.
    My guess: _____

7. Blue jeans were first made as <u>rugged</u> clothes for people who have to work hard.
    My guess: _____

Listen

3 **Listening for Main Ideas.**   Listen to the conversation. As you listen, answer these questions.

1. What are David, Beth, and Ali enjoying?

2. What happened to the car?

3. Who is going to help David?

4 **Listening for Specific Information.**   Listen again. This time, listen for the answers to these questions.

1. Where did Beth, David, and Ali go last summer?

2. How is Kyoto different from the Grand Canyon?

3. Which place do they say is old? Which place is new?

4. What does David do after he discovers the flat tire?

After You Listen

5   **Understanding Main Ideas.**   Work with a partner. Decide which of the words below describe Kyoto, Japan, and which describe the Grand Canyon in the United States. Some words may describe both places. Write the words in the correct column on the chart. Add a few words of your own.

Cherry blossoms

Grand Canyon at dawn

gentle	wild	rugged	calm
beautiful	old	hard	mountainous
traditional	dry	colorful	uncrowded

Kyoto	Grand Canyon

Stress

6 **Listening for Stressed Words.**   Listen to the first part of the conversation again.

1.   The stressed words are missing. Fill in the blanks with words from the list.

beautiful	Grand Canyon	like	rugged
cherry blossoms	great	old	think
day	history	peaceful	traditions
different	Japan	place	wild

Beth: What a _____ _____ to be out driving. These

⁣   1   2

_____ are _____!

⁣   3   4

Ali: Yes, I _____ I _____ it even more than that

⁣   5   6

_____ we visited last summer — the _____.

⁣   7   8

David: The Grand Canyon was very _____ — you know,

⁣   9

_____ and _____. This is so _____.

⁣   10   11   12

Ali: Well, _____ is a very _____ country with a

⁣   13   14

long _____ and many _____.

⁣   15   16

2.   Now read the conversation with a partner. Practice stressing words correctly.

7 **Stress and Word Families.**   In word families, related nouns, verbs, and adjectives often differ mostly in stress.

1.   Listen to the word families below. Repeat each word after the speaker.

1.	photógraphy (n.)	phótograph (n. and v.)	photográphic (adj.)
2.	récord (n.)	recórd (v.)	
3.	désert (n.)		desérted (adj.)
4.	bénefit (n.)		benefícial (adj.)
5.	advertísement (n.)	ádvertise (v.)	
6.	análysis (n.)	ánalyze (v.)	
7.	examinátion(n.)	exámine (v.)	
8.	educátion (n.)	éducate (v.)	

2.   Listen to the sentences. Mark the stress of the underlined word.

   1.   <u>Photography</u> is a popular hobby.
   2.   The <u>desert</u> is a bad place to have a flat tire.
   3.   I keep good <u>records</u> of my income and expenses.
   4.   The medicine had a <u>beneficial</u> effect on the patient.
   5.   I have class tonight, so please <u>record</u> my favorite TV program for me.
   6.   You must pass the <u>examination</u> to pass the course.
   7.   Schools try to <u>educate</u> every student equally.
   8.   I need to <u>analyze</u> the results of my research.
   9.   I saw the <u>advertisement</u> in the newspaper.
   10.   Please take a <u>photograph</u> of us in front of the monument.

Talk It Over

1.   Look at the photos. Make a sentence describing one of the photos.

   Example: Many people visit this place every year to ski.

2.   Your classmates will guess which picture you are describing.
3.   Then listen to their sentences and try to guess which picture they are describing.

PART 2	# Listening Skills

Getting Meaning from Context

1 **Vocabulary Preview.**   David, Beth, and Ali are on another trip. This time they are in the Southwestern United States. Listen. Circle the words you don't know.

Nouns		**Verb**	**Adjective**
trunk	luggage	(to) take up space	freezing
tent	flash flood		
sleeping bag	advisory		
fishing equipment			

2 **Using Context Clues.**

1. Listen to the first part of each conversation.
2. Listen to the question and circle the letter of the best answer.
3. Then listen to the last part to hear the correct answer.

1. What did Beth, David, and Ali finish doing?

    a.   changing a flat tire

    b.   putting everything in the car

    c.   taking everything out of the car

2. What are Ali, David, and Beth going to do?

    a.   eat a picnic lunch in the desert

    b.   look at a map

    c.   find a restaurant

3. Why is David going to turn on the radio?

    a. to listen to some music

    b. to hear a weather report

    c. to find something to listen to

4. What's the weather probably going to be like tonight?

    a. rainy and hot

    b. cloudy and cool

    c. rainy and cold

5. Why is David sorry?

    a. He didn't see the motel sign.

    b. He didn't want to go camping in the rain.

    c. He didn't see a stop sign.

Listening to a Tour Guide

Before You Listen

3 **Preparing to Listen.** Before you listen, talk about sightseeing with a partner.

1. Do you like to go sightseeing?

2. What city in the world do you think is good for sightseeing?

3. What are some interesting sights to see in your hometown or your city?

4 **Vocabulary Preview.** Match the expressions on the left with the pictures on the right.

____*b*____ 1. interstate highway

_____ 2. capitol building

_____ 3. a Civil War general

_____ 4. amusement park

_____ 5. roller coaster

_____ 6. a grave

Listen

5 **Listening for Main Ideas.**   You are going to go on a sightseeing tour of a major U.S. city. As you listen to the tour guide, answer these questions.

1.   What state are you in?

2.   What city are you touring?

6 **Listening for Places on a Map.**   Listen again. As you hear the description of each place, write its number in the correct spot on the map.

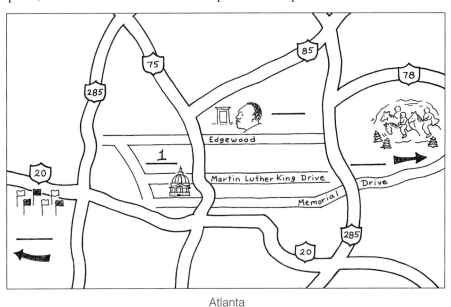

Atlanta

7 **Listening to a Tour Guide.**   Listen again. Next to the name of each place below, write a few words describing it.

1.   The Capitol building _____

_____

2.   Martin Luther King Jr. National Historic Site _____

_____

3.   Stone Mountain _____

_____

4.   Six Flags Amusement Park _____

_____

Listening for Flight Information

Before You Listen

8 **Preparing to Listen.** Before you listen, discuss these questions in small groups.

1. When did you last (most recently) take a plane trip?
2. Where did you go?
3. Did you enjoy the trip? Why or why not?

9 **Vocabulary Preview.** Listen to these words and expressions. Circle the ones you don't know.

Nouns	Verbs	Adjectives
round trip	(to) depart	round trip (ticket)
one way	(to) change planes	one way (ticket)
first class	(to) arrive	nonrefundable
business class		nonstop
coach class		direct

Listen

10 **Listening for the Main Idea.** Alicia is planning a trip to Disney World in Florida. She needs help to plan her trip. Where is Alicia? Circle the number of the correct picture.

Picture 1

Picture 2

11   **Listening for Flight Information.**   Listen again. Answer these questions.

1.   What kind of ticket does Alicia want to buy?

   a.   first class

   b.   coach class

   c.   business class

2.   When does Alicia's flight leave?

   a.   on Saturday afternoon

   b.   on Sunday evening

   c.   on Sunday morning

3.   Why doesn't Alicia want the nonstop, direct flight?

   a.   She wants to visit Chicago.

   b.   It's much more expensive.

   c.   It takes longer.

4.   Why is Alicia's ticket nonrefundable?

   a.   It's a special low fare.

   b.   It's nonstop.

   c.   She's going coach.

After You Listen

12   **Discussing Flight Information.**   Discuss the following questions in small groups.

1.   Have you ever used a travel agent to plan a trip?

2.   Which would you rather do?

   a.   Pay more for a nonstop flight (or express train) to arrive sooner.

   b.   Pay more for a nonstop flight so you don't have to change planes.

   c.   Save money by taking a longer flight (or trip) and changing planes (or trains).

3.   How long in advance do you usually plan a trip?

| **PART 3** | # Reading |

Before You Read

1   Look at this photo. In small groups, discuss these questions.
1.   What are these people doing?
2.   What do you like to do on a vacation?

2   **Vocabulary Preview.**   We often use *go* + *-ing* to describe activities we do for pleasure. For example, we use *go* + *swimming* to describe the complete activity of going to a place and swimming. Rather than saying "Let's swim" to suggest the activity, we say "Let's go swimming." We also often add the verb *be* + *going to* before *go* + *-ing*: "We're going to go swimming." This expresses an action that will take place in the future.

Example:
The verb *swim* means "to use one's body to move through the water." But if someone asks you, "What are you going to do tomorrow?" you probably wouldn't say, "I'm going to swim." Instead you would answer, I'm going to ___go swimming___.

Complete the following sentences. Then check your answers with a partner.

1.   The verb *camp* means "to live for a while in a temporary place, usually in a tent." But if someone asks you, "What are going to do this summer?" you would answer, "I'm going to _____."

2.   The verb *sightsee* means "to take a trip to a place and look around," in other words, to "see the sights at a place that a person specially travels to." But if someone asks you, "What are you going to do in Mexico?" you would probably answer, _____.

Here are some other common verbs with *go* — *go hiking, go walking, go jogging, go boating, go surfing, go bowling, go window-shopping, go fishing*. If you don't know the meanings of some of these verbs, ask a classmate or your teacher. Then work with a partner and practice using these verbs in sentences.

3 **Making Good Guesses.** Remember that sometimes you can understand new words without a dictionary. For example, you can figure out or guess the meanings from other words in the sentence. Guess the meaning of the underlined words. Circle the letter to complete the sentence.

1. When I visited London I went to the Tate Museum, but there were so many other <u>tourists</u> there, I couldn't see anything. It was hot and crowded.
   Tourists are most likely _____.
   a. police officers
   b. sightseers
   c. art experts

2. Many things cause <u>pollution</u>—for example, factory smoke, car exhaust, trash, and garbage.
   Pollution is most likely _____.
   a. rain and bad weather
   b. a lot of new business
   c. bad things in the air and environment

3. The mountain was really a <u>volcano</u>. Twenty years ago smoke and fire poured out of the top of the mountain.
   A *volcano* is most likely a _____.
   a. mountain with ice at the top
   b. mountain with a hole in the top
   c. mountain that is very tall

Read

4 Read the article. Try to guess the meanings of new words.

Adventure Vacations

A People like different kinds of vacations. Some go camping. They swim, fish, cook over a fire, and sleep outside. Others like to stay at a hotel in an exciting city. They go shopping all day and go dancing all night. Or maybe they go sightseeing to places such as Disneyland, the Taj Mahal, or the Louvre.

B Some people are bored with sightseeing trips. They don't want to be "tourists." They want to have an adventure—a surprising and exciting trip. They want to learn something and maybe help people too. How can they do this? Some travel companies and environmental groups are planning special adventures. Sometimes these trips are difficult and full of hardships, but they're a lot of fun. One organization, Earthwatch, sends small groups of volunteers to different parts of the world. Some volunteers spend two weeks and study the environment. Others work with animals. Others learn about people of the past.

C | Would you like an adventure in the Far North? A team of volunteers is leaving from Murmansk, Russia. The leader of this trip is a professor from Alaska. He's worried about chemicals from factories. He and the volunteers will study this pollution in the environment. If you like exercise and cold weather, this is a good trip for you. Volunteers need to ski sixteen kilometers every day.

D | Do you enjoy ocean animals? You can spend two to four weeks in Hawaii. There, you can teach language to dolphins. Dolphins can follow orders such as "Bring me the large ball." They also understand opposites. How much more can they understand? It will be exciting to learn about these intelligent animals. Another study trip goes to Washington State and follows orcas. We call orcas "killer whales," but they're really dolphins—the largest kind of dolphin. These beautiful animals travel together in family groups. They move through the ocean with their mothers, grandmothers, and great-grandmothers. Ocean pollution is changing their lives. Earthwatch is studying how this happens.

E | Are you interested in history? Then Greece is the place for your adventure. Thirty-five hundred years ago a volcano exploded there, on Santorini. This explosion was more terrible than Krakatoa or Mount Saint Helens. But today we know a lot about the way of life of the people from that time. There are houses, kitchens, and paintings as interesting as those in Pompeii. Today teams of volunteers are learning more about people from the past.

F | Do you want a very different vacation? Do you want to travel far, work hard, and learn a lot? Then an Earthwatch vacation is for you.

After You Read

5 **Finding the Main Ideas.**   Circle the number of the main idea of "Adventure Vacations."

1. An adventure with Earthwatch is a good way to learn something and have a vacation too.
2. It's more fun to stay at a hotel than to go camping.
3. Disneyland, the Taj Mahal, and the Louvre are wonderful places to see on a vacation.
4. Earthwatch trips are difficult and full of hardships.

Here are the main ideas of paragraphs A to D. What information about the main idea is in each paragraph? Put checks on the lines.

A: People like different kinds of vacations.

____✔____ Some people go camping.

_____ Some people swim, fish, cook over a fire, and sleep outside.

_____ Some people stay at a hotel in a city.

_____ Some people learn about neighborhood problems.

_____ Some people go shopping and dancing.

_____ Some people go to special places such as Disneyland.

B: Some people want an adventure.

_____ They want to stay at a hotel and go shopping.

_____ They want to learn something and maybe help people too.

_____ Some groups plan special adventures.

_____ Earthwatch sends volunteers to different places in the world.

_____ Earthwatch volunteers help in shelters for the homeless.

_____ Earthwatch volunteers study the environment, work with animals, and learn about people of the past.

C: A group of volunteers is going to study pollution in the arctic.

_____ The leader is a professor from Murmansk.

_____ The professor is worried about chemicals.

_____ People on this trip will go camping.

_____ People on this trip will ski sixteen kilometers every day.

D: You can teach dolphins in Hawaii or study orcas in Washington.

_____ Dolphins can follow orders.

_____ Dolphins understand opposites.

_____ Dolphins are intelligent.

_____ Dolphins are fish.

_____ Orcas travel in family groups.

_____ Pollution is changing the lives of orcas.

6 **Making Good Guesses.**   Circle the correct letter to complete the sentence.

The writer probably _____.

a.   likes to go sightseeing

b.   likes adventures

c.   teaches language to dolphins

Discussing the Reading

7 Talk about your answers in small groups.

1.   What do you like to do for fun in your free time?
2.   Do you sometimes go camping? If so, where?
3.   Do you like to go shopping, dancing, or sightseeing? If so, where?
4.   Do you enjoy museums? If so, which ones do you like?
5.   Would you like an adventure? If so, what kind of adventure? Are any of the adventures in paragraphs C, D, and E interesting to you? Why, or why not?

PART 4

Writing

Using Verb Tenses and Adjectives

Read the letter and look at the picture. Find examples of pine trees, rocks, and islands in the picture. Then answer the questions. Share your answers with a partner.

1.   What activities does the writer talk about?
2.   What can the writer see around him?

Dear Bill,
I'm here in Brunswick, Maine, a small town
on the coast. My log cabin is old and weathered.
Huge waves roll and crash against the jagged rocks.
I can see beautiful green islands out in the bay.
Tall and fresh-smelling pine trees are all around me.
    I'm reading a lot, swimming, and relaxing. I went
fishing yesterday and caught a dogfish (that's a
small shark). See you soon.

                                    Jim

Adjectives make descriptions "come alive" (become interesting). The secret to good writing is to use only important, interesting adjectives that make a strong picture in the reader's mind. For example, compare the following two descriptions:

My log cabin is *old* and *weathered*.
Tall and *fresh-smelling* pine trees are all around me.

Notice that the adjectives help the reader form a picture in his or her mind. Sometimes no adjectives are better than boring adjectives.

Along the shore there were big rocks and green pine trees.

Notice that *big* and *green* do not add very much to the writer's picture of the rocks and pine trees because we already know that rocks are usually big and pine trees are green.

Practicing the Writing Process

1   **Exploring Ideas: Free Writing.**   Write for ten minutes. Imagine you are on a great vacation. Write down a list of things you will do and see. Write at least seven things you can see. Don't worry about spelling or grammar.

2   **Writing the First Draft.**   Write a postcard or a short letter. Tell where you are, what you are doing, and what you can see, hear, and smell at your vacation place.

3   **Editing.**   Notice the verb tenses in the short letter from Jim—the present tense ("I'm here"), the present continuous tense for the actions that are continuing ("I'm reading a lot"), and the simple past tense for the actions that happened and are finished ("I went fishing"). Review your letter and check all the tenses. Did you use them correctly?

     Use the following checklist to correct any mistakes.

Editing Checklist

1.   Does every subject have a verb?

2.   Do your sentences begin with capital letters?

3.   Do other words in the writing need capital letters?

4.   Do your sentences end with periods or other final punctuation?

4   **Peer Editing.**   Show your letter to another student. Read and discuss each other's work.

5   **Writing the Second Draft.**   Now write the second draft of your letter. Be sure to include interesting adjectives. When you're finished, give your letter to your teacher.

Writing a Journal

6   Here is a journal entry written by Jim, the same person who wrote the short letter. Notice that this is a narrative—it uses only the past tense.

June 25, 2001

    Today I had a great day. I sat on the porch of the house. From there I could see out across the bay. Along the shore there were rocks and pines trees. The islands looked like round, green bumps where the sky met the bay.

    I sat in an old pine porch chair with my feet up on the porch railing. The breeze from the ocean felt cool against my face. I read a little, then I looked out on the water, then I read a little more. Everything made me feel alive and happy—the sharp smell of the pines, the crisp feel of the ocean breeze, the very blue sky and ocean. I wanted the morning to last forever.

Write a journal entry about one day on a vacation that you took. Use the simple past tense. What details can you include to make a stronger picture in the reader's mind?

| PART 5 | # Grammar |

A. Adjectives with *-ing* and *-ed*

Adjectives with *-ing* and *-ed* often follow *to be*.

	Examples		Notes
Giver The movie **excited**	Receiver Josh.	The movie was **excit*ing*.** Josh was **excit*ed*.**	Use *-ing* with the *giver* of a feeling.
Giver Dave **bores**	Receiver Michelle.	Dave is **bor*ing*.** Michelle is **bor*ed*.**	Use *-ed* with the *receiver* of a feeling.

1   Here's one thing Josh and I agree on. It's fun to watch people, especially in our classes. It's entertaining, and it doesn't cost anything!

Look at the pictures below. Then answer the questions using the *-ing* or *-ed* forms of the adjectives.

Example: Who is bored?
The students are bored.

1. Who is bored?
    Who is boring?

2. Who is interesting?
    Who is interested?

3. Who was fascinated?
    Who was fascinating?

4. Who was disappointed?
    What was disappointing?

5. Who is surprised?
    What is surprising?

6. Is the book confusing or confused?
    Is Harry confusing or confused?

B. Comparative Adjectives

Comparatives show how two things are different. The form of the comparative depends on how many syllables the adjective has.

	Examples	Notes
One-syllable adjectives	France isn't **cheap**. Italy is **cheaper than** France.	Add *-er* to one syllable adjectives. Use *than* to show the other choice.
Adjectives that end in -*y*	French isn't **easy**. Italian is **easier** to learn **than** French.	When adjectives end in *y*, change the *y* to *i* and add *-er*.

2 You and your friend are going to visit both France and Italy. Which cities should you visit? Study the map of France and use your imagination. Then use the adjectives to make sentences comparing the cities.

Example: cool
Paris is cooler than Nice.

1. warm

2. noisy

3. green

4. big

5. small

6. close (to the ocean)

7. sunny

8. cloudy

9. near (to England)

_____

_____

_____

_____

_____

_____

_____

_____

_____

C. More Comparative Adjectives

Longer adjectives use *more...than* to form the comparative.

	Examples	Notes
Two-syllable adjectives that don't end in -y	This map is **more helpful than** that one. She is **more tired than** Jack.	Use *more...than* with these adjectives. Don't add *-er*.
Adjectives with more than two syllables	The mountains are **more beautiful than** the beach.	Use *more...than* with these adjectives. Don't add *-er*.

3 Which Italian cities should you and your friend visit? Read what the travel agent says. Then use the adjectives below to make sentences comparing Florence and Rome.

Example: beautiful

Florence is more beautiful than Rome.

Rome is important, exciting, and interesting, but it is also crowded.

Florence is beautiful, relaxing, peaceful, and safe, but it is also very expensive.

1. exciting
2. safe
3. expensive
4. important
5. relaxing

6. interesting
7. crowded
8. peaceful
9. enjoyable

D. Superlatives with Adjectives and Adverbs

Use superlatives to compare three or more people or things. Use *the* with superlatives.

	Examples	**Notes**
One-syllable adjectives and adverbs	I am **the fastest** runner on our team. Joe runs **the slowest** of anyone.	Add *-est* to one-syllable adjectives and adverbs.
Two-syllable adjectives ending in *y*	Jack is **the laziest** person on the team.	Add *-est* to two-syllable adjectives ending in *y*.
Longer adjectives and adverbs	Watching TV is **the most interesting** thing to do. Esther skis **the most dangerously** of anyone.	Use *the most* with multisyllable adjectives (not ending in *y*). Use *the most* with all multisyllable adverbs.
Irregulars	Janis skis **the best** of anyone I know. She is **the worst** student in our school.	The superlative form of *good* is *best*. The superlative form of *bad* is *worst*.

4   Hi, I'm Esther. Last week I saw these three actors on late-night movies. Use the pictures and your imagination to answer the questions. Use the superlative in your answers.

Vern   Gary   George

Example: Who is the most handsome of the three?

(I think that) Gary is the most handsome (of the three).

1. Who looks the strongest?
2. Who looks the most intelligent?
3. Who looks the dumbest?
4. Who is the most athletic?
5. Who is the youngest?
6. Who is the heaviest?
7. Who is the best actor?
8. Who is the worst actor?

Video Activities: Cancun

Before You Watch.

1. The resort city of Cancun is in _____.
   a. Spain   b. Thailand   c. Mexico

2. What activity do people usually not do at a beach resort?
   a. visit museums   c. go scuba diving
   b. go swimming   d. go sailing

Watch.

1. Most activities in Cancun are on the _____.
   a. water   b. beach   c. island

2. Check the things that you can do in Cancun:

   _____ parasail   _____ go in a submarine

   _____ scuba dive   _____ swim with turtles

   _____ take a helicopter ride   _____ snorkel

   _____ ride in a glass-bottom boat   _____ meet famous people

   _____ visit Isla Mujeres

Watch Again.

Complete the sentences with the numbers in the box.

10	20	25	2	30	2 to 3

1. Isla Mujeres is about _____ miles from Cancun. It takes about _____ minutes to get there by boat. The boat ride costs $_____.

2. You can go parasailing in Cancun. It costs about $_____ to parasail for _____ minutes.

3. Party boats are not expensive. For about $_____ you can have lunch and go snorkeling.

After You Watch.

Discuss these questions in small groups. What makes you choose a place for a vacation? Why?

a. good museums   d. chance to practice another language
b. good shopping   e. chance to meet interesting people
c. exciting activities

Now imagine you are in Cancun. Write a postcard to a friend. Describe Cancun to your friend. Then tell your friend what you did yesterday, what you are doing now and what you are going to do tomorrow.

Chapter 10

Our Planet

IN THIS CHAPTER

Listening
- Listening for main ideas and specific information
- Listening for stressed words and reductions
- Getting meaning from context
- Listening to persuasive messages

Speaking
- Identifying information requested through emphasized words in a question

Reading
- Previewing vocabulary
- Identifying main ideas
- Identifying specific information
- Using context clues to understand new words

- Reading an expository piece about the greenhouse effect
- Drawing conclusions

Writing
- Analyzing a composition
- Using the writing process
- Writing a problem / solution composition
- Editing for composition development, verb forms, capitalization and punctuation, and spelling

Grammar
- Regular and irregular past participles
- The present perfect tense
- The passive voice with simple tenses

| **PART 1** | # Listening to Conversations |

Before You Listen

1   Preparing to Listen.   Discuss these photos in small groups.

1.   Describe Photo 1. What kind of pollution does it show?
2.   Describe Photo 2. What kind of pollution does it show?
3.   Which kind of pollution do you think is more serious?
4.   What kinds of things are people doing to fight pollution?

2   Vocabulary Preview.   Lee is visiting Alicia.

1.   Listen to these words from their conversation. Circle the ones you don't know.

Nouns	**Verbs**	**Expression**
pollution	to pollute	to give a speech
environment	to clean up	
oil refineries	to pick up	

2.   Guess the meanings of the underlined words. Write your guess on the lines. Check your answers with a dictionary or your teacher.

1.   Nowadays the air in many cities is very dirty. Cars and factories cause this air <u>pollution</u>.

My guess: _____

2.   We live on the earth. It is our natural <u>environment</u>.

My guess: _____

3. I'm going <u>to give a speech</u> to the class. I'm going to talk about the planet and pollution in front of the class.

   My guess: _____

4. People don't want cars and factories <u>to pollute</u> the air. We need clean, not dirty, air.

   My guess: _____

5. You <u>pick up</u> the trash from the ground. Put it in this trash can. I'll wash the tables and chairs. We can <u>clean up</u> this area of the park quickly.

   My guess (pick up): _____

   My guess: (clean up) _____

6. We visited an <u>oil refinery</u> last year. It's interesting to see how they take oil from the ground and make it into gasoline and other petroleum products.

   My guess: _____

Listen

3 **Listening for Main Ideas.** Listen to the conversation. As you listen, answer these questions.

1. What is Alicia doing?
2. On Earth Day, what do people think about?
3. Who is going to give a speech?
4. Why does Lee want to help?

4 **Listening for Specific Information.** Listen again. This time, fill in the chart below with the Earth Day activities you hear.

Place	Earth Day Activities
Washington, D.C.	People marched. They asked for new laws.
Italy	
Africa	
Japan	
Faber College	

After You Listen

5 **Understanding Main Ideas.**   Circle the letter of the correct answer.

1.   What is the main purpose of Earth Day?
    a.   for people to exercise by riding bicycles
    b.   for people to think about the earth and the environment
    c.   for people to travel to places around the world

2.   When did Earth Day start?
    a.   one year ago
    b.   ten years ago
    c.   more than 30 years ago

3.   What kind of pollution do people think about on Earth Day?
    a.   air pollution
    b.   water pollution
    c.   both a and b

4.   What are Alicia and Lee going to do on Earth Day?
    a.   give a speech and carry signs
    b.   go to Washington, D. C. to protest
    c.   clean up a park

6 **Vocabulary Review.**   Complete these sentences. Use words from the list.

pollution	to pollute	to give a speech
environment	to clean up	
oil refineries	to pick (something) up	

1.   Cars are one of the biggest sources of air _____.

2.   Please don't throw trash on the ground. Please _____ it _____ and put it in the trash can.

3.   I want to tell people about water pollution but I'm afraid _____ _____ _____ _____ in public.

4.   Some factories _____ the air more than others.

5.   I need some water and soap to _____ _____ _____ the floor in the kitchen.

6.   What laws do we need to protect the _____ from air and water pollution?

7.   You can see the smoke from the _____ _____ for miles and miles.

Stress

7 **Listening for Stressed Words.**   Listen to the first part of the conversation again.

1. Some of the stressed words are missing. Fill in the blanks with words from the list.

April	heard	Monday	sign
doing	Hi	people	start
Earth Day	in	pollution	that
environment	is	problems	
first	making	Really	

Alicia: Come _____!
                                    1

Lee: _____, Alicia. What are you _____?
                    2   3

Alicia: Hi, Lee. I'm _____ a _____ for
                                            4   5

           _____.
                      6

Lee: Earth Day? What's _____?
                                              7

Alicia: On Earth Day, _____ think about _____
                                            8   9

           and other _____ with the _____.
                                  10   11

Lee: _____! When _____ Earth Day?
                    12   13

Alicia: Next _____.
                              14

Lee: I've never _____ of Earth Day. When did it
                                  15

           _____?
                      16

Alicia: The _____ Earth Day was on _____ 22, 1970.
                              17   18

           A U.S. senator and a college student started it. They wanted

           people to be more aware of problems with the environment.

2. Now read the conversation with a partner. Practice stressing words correctly.

Talk It Over

Work with a partner. Add Alicia's response to each dialogue. Pay attention to the emphasis in Lee's question. What information does he want? Role-play your dialogues.

Alicia: Some people think air pollution is a big problem, but others think progress is more important.

Lee: Well, what do *you* think about pollution?

Alicia: I agree that it's a big problem. Progress is no good if we don't have clean air to breathe.

Alicia: Air pollution and water pollution are two serious environmental problems.

Lee: Do you think *air pollution* is the biggest problem?

Alicia: _____

Alicia: One of the things I do on Earth Day is to stop driving my car.

Lee: Will you ride your *bicycle* to school on Earth Day?

Alicia: _____

Alicia: We're going to plant trees all over town on Earth Day. We have 500 trees to plant.

Lee: How many trees will you plant on *campus*?

Alicia: _____

Alicia: Students from the college are going to clean up Audubon Park, Haley Park, Finley Park, and Tom Lee Park.

Lee: Which parks are *you* going to clean up?

Alicia: _____

PART 2 Listening Skills

Getting Meaning from Context

1 Using Context Clues.   Different people are discussing local and global problems.

1. Listen to each speaker.
2. Listen to the question and write the number of the speaker next to the answer.
3. Then listen to the speaker again to hear the correct answer.

____ air pollution   ____ water pollution

____ crime   ____ overcrowding (too many people)

____ traffic problems   ____ the environment

Listening to Persuasive Messages

Before You Listen

2 **Preparing to Listen.**   Before you listen, discuss these questions with a partner or in a small group.

1. What do people do in their everyday lives to contribute to pollution and other environmental problems?
2. Do you personally do anything to help the environment?

3 **Vocabulary Preview.**   Listen to these words and phrases. Circle the ones you don't know.

Nouns	Verbs	Adjectives
shuttle bus	to recycle	mature
faucet		slaughtered
topsoil		veggie
species		
toxic chemicals		
recyclables		
carbon dioxide		
endangered species		

Listen

4 **Listening for the Main Idea.**   Listen to the following messages.

1. As you listen, try to answer this question.
       Where might you hear these messages?
2. Listen again. This time write the number of the message next to the main point of the message.

_____ a. Save water.

_____ b. Don't eat meat.

_____ c. Don't drive your car.

_____ d. Recycle—don't throw things away.

_____ e. Eat food without chemicals.

5 **Listening for Specific Information.** Listen again. This time, match each of the main messages with the details about how you can help or hurt the environment.

Main Message

1. Save water

2. Don't eat meat.

3. Don't drive your car.

4. Recycle—don't throw things away.

5. Eat food without chemicals.

Details

a. Raising cattle for meat uses a lot of water, topsoil, and other resources.
b. It's better to recycle your trash than to throw it away.
c. Cars pollute the air.
d. Animals raised for meat contain toxic chemicals.
e. Trees produce oxygen to replace polluted air.
f. Raising cattle for meat adds carbon dioxide to the air.
g. Brushing your teeth wastes a lot of water.
h. Burgers made from vegetables are better for the environment than burgers made from meat.

After You Listen

6 **Discussing Main Ideas.** Answer these questions in small groups.

1. Do you agree with any of the main messages from the announcements of the Earth Fair? Which ones?
2. If you disagree with any of the main messages, tell your group why you disagree.
3. Do the members of your group do anything to help the environment? On the chart, list what actions you do in each of the following areas.

Goals	Actions your group takes
1. Reduce air pollution from cars.	
2. Save water.	
3. Recycle glass, paper, cans, etc.	
4. Reduce use of toxic chemicals	
5. Other environmental issues	

| PART 3 | # Reading |

Before You Read

1 Look at these pictures. In small groups, answer the following questions.

1. Why did someone cut down the trees in Picture A? How will people use these trees?
2. What problem is the factory causing?
3. There are five kinds of energy in the pictures in B. Which kinds of energy do people use in your country?

A

B

    oil   coal   sun

    wind   water

2   **Vocabulary Preview.**   Read the following sentences to help understand the meanings of the underlined words. Then answer the questions. Don't use a dictionary.

1. Factories send <u>gases</u> such as CO_2 into the atmosphere.
    What is one example of a gas? _____

2. Factories send gases such as CO_2 into the <u>atmosphere</u>, the air around the earth.
    What is the atmosphere? _____

3. Trees <u>absorbed</u>, or drank in, CO_2.
    What does *absorb* mean? _____

4. We should learn to use different kinds of <u>energy</u>: the sun, wind, and heat from volcanoes.
    What are three examples of energy? _____

5. There is too much CO_2, and there aren't enough trees, so the world is getting warmer. In other words, we have a <u>greenhouse effect</u>.
    What happens in a greenhouse effect? _____

Read

3   Read the article. Try to understand the meanings of new words without using a dictionary.

The Greenhouse Effect and the Women of Guatemala

A   Most people know something about the greenhouse effect. Factories send gases such as carbon dioxide, or CO_2, into the atmosphere, the air around the earth. In the past, this wasn't a problem because trees absorbed, or drank in, CO_2. But now people are cutting down billions of trees in many countries. At the same time, factories are sending more CO_2 into the atmosphere. It's difficult to believe, but factories put billions of tons of CO_2 into the atmosphere every year! One ton is 2,000 pounds, so this is a lot of pollution. There is too much CO_2, and there aren't enough trees, so the world is getting warmer. In other words, we have a greenhouse effect. This is terrible for the environment.

B   What can we do about this? First, we can stop using so much coal and oil. We can learn to use different kinds of energy: the sun, wind, and heat from volcanoes and from inside the earth. Second, instead of cutting down trees, we should plant more trees. One tree can absorb ten pounds of carbon dioxide every year.

C   In the past, the mountains of Guatemala, in Central America, were green and thick with beautiful trees. But people cut down trees for houses. Also, many women cook over wood fires. They walk hours every day to look for firewood. There are fewer and fewer trees, and this is bad for the land. Rain washes good soil down the mountains.

D   Far away from Guatemala, in the state of Connecticut, there is a new factory. The factory uses coal. It will send 400,000 tons of CO_2 into the atmosphere every year. Many people are angry about this. But the factory owners are doing something about it. They are giving two million dollars to the women of Guatemala. The Guatemalans will plant trees in their country. These trees in Central America will absorb the carbon dioxide from the factory in Connecticut.

E   Why Guatemala? Why don't people in Connecticut plant the trees in Connecticut? The answer is easy. Trees grow much faster in Central America than in the northern part of the United States.

F   The trees are good for the earth's atmosphere. They're good for Guatemala too. In small towns and villages in Guatemala, most women are poor and have hard lives. Trees help them in three ways. First, the Connecticut factory pays them to plant the trees. Their pay is corn, not money. The corn is food for their children. Second, these women know a lot about their environment. They know where to plant, when to plant, and what kinds of trees to plant. For example, they plant many fruit trees. The fruit gives them vitamins in their families' diets. Other trees are good for firewood. In a few years, the women won't spend so much time walking for wood. Third, all these trees are good for the soil. Now rain can't wash the soil down the mountains so easily.

G   This plan isn't enough to stop the greenhouse effect. But it's a beginning. The women of Guatemala are helping themselves and helping their environment. As one woman says, "We're planting for our families, for our children."

After You Read

4 **Finding the Main Ideas.**   Circle the number of the main idea of the article.

1.   The greenhouse effect is a problem in the world today.
2.   We should stop using coal and oil and use other kinds of energy.
3.   A new U.S. factory is making people angry because it uses coal.
4.   Women in Guatemala are planting trees, and these trees are helping the women's families and the environment.

Which information from the article explains the main idea? Write the information in the boxes.

Main Idea: Trees are good for people and the environment.

5 Read the following sentences. If the information is not in the article, cross out the sentence. If the information is given, which sentence from the article has the information? Write the sentence.

1. Trees absorb carbon dioxide.

    One tree can absorb ten pounds of carbon dioxide every year.
    _____

2. All trees are beautiful.
    _____
    _____

3. Trees give people fruit.
    _____
    _____

4. Trees need too much water.
    _____
    _____

5. Trees give people wood for fires.
    _____
    _____

6. Trees are good for the land.
    _____
    _____

6 **Making Good Guesses.**   Which fact can you guess from the article? Circle the letter of the answer.

a. Trees are important.
b. Connecticut is in the western part of the United States.
c. The women of Guatemala are rich now.

Discussing the Reading

7 Discuss your answers to the following questions with a group.

1. Are there many trees in your neighborhood? In your country?

2. What kinds of energy are important in the United States? What kinds of energy are important in your country? What environmental problems do you have in your country?

PART 4	# Writing

Analyzing a Composition

Read the student's problem / solution composition.

Paragraph 1: Introduction to the problem

One important problem in Los Angeles is the traffic. It has serious consequences, not only for the environment, but for people's well-being.

Paragraph 2: Details and facts about the problem

People own more than 5 million cars in the LA area, and it often seems as if all of them are always on the road. Someone estimated that people in Los Angeles spend 1.2 billion hours in their cars. Every morning and evening, movement on the freeways nearly stops. Even at strange hours like 10:00 at night, the traffic may suddenly stop.

Paragraph 3: One possible solution

Los Angeles just completed a subway, but this is not going to be a solution to the problem. People don't use it. They like their cars better. They want to be in control and drive exactly where they want. What can be done to change people's minds?

Paragraph 4: The writer's solution

In Singapore, drivers must pay extra money for using the freeways during the most popular hours. A computer system automatically charges cars. Los Angeles should build a system like this. The money that is charged can be used to build other kinds of transportation like more subways and improved buses.

Paragraph 5: Conclusion

The traffic problem in Los Angeles is becoming worse every day. We need a solution right now.

Can you think of a good title for this composition? Compare your answer with a partner's.

Practicing the Writing Process

1   **Exploring Ideas: Free Writing.**   You are going to write a problem / solution composition. Review the composition about Los Angeles traffic. Write down facts and details about the problem. Then write possible solutions. Don't worry about grammar, spelling, or punctuation.

2   **Writing the First Draft.**   Now write your first draft. Begin by completing the following topic sentence. Use the words in parentheses as a guide.

One important problem in my _____(place)_____ is

_____(the problem)_____.

To help you organize your paragraphs, look carefully at how the composition about Los Angeles traffic is organized. If you are writing this composition as a homework assignment, you should include facts and statistics about the problem. You can do this by using library references or the Internet. If you are writing in class, you probably will not be able to include facts and statistics, but you still can add examples and other information that you know.

3   **Editing.**   Here's a list of things to check in your composition.

Editing Checklist

1.   Is there an introduction, development paragraphs, and a conclusion?

2.   Is there a title?

3.   Are the verb forms correct?

4.   Do your sentences begin with capital letters?

5.   Do other words in the writing need capital letters?

6.   Do your sentences end with periods or other final punctuation?

7.   Is your spelling correct?

4   **Peer Editing.**   Show your composition to another student. Read and discuss each other's work.

5   **Writing the Second Draft.**   Write your second draft and give it to your teacher.

PART 5	# Grammar

A. Past Participles

For regular verbs, the past participle is the same as the simple past tense (verb + *ed*):

Simple Form	Simple Past and Past Participle
call study	called studied

For irregular verbs, the past participle often changes spelling and / or pronunciation. Here is a short list of irregular past participles.

Simple Forms	Past Participles	Simple Forms	Past Participles
be	been	make	made
become	become	mean	meant
begin	begun	meet	met
buy	bought	pay	paid
choose	chosen	read	read
do	done	ride	rode
eat	eaten	say	said
feed	fed	see	seen
fight	fought	speak	spoken
get	gotten	spend	spent
give	given	take	taken
have	had	think	thought
hear	heard	understand	understood
hold	held	win	won
know	known	write	written
leave	left		

B. Present Perfect Tense: Affirmative and Negative Statements

The present perfect tense has several uses. A common use is to talk about actions in the past when we don't say or know the specific time. With the present perfect, no specific past time expression is used. Compare: *She has lived in Boston* (present perfect). *She lived in Boston last year* (simple past with a specific time).

Affirmative	Negative
I / you / we / they **have worked** there.	I / you / we / they **haven't worked** there.
She / he / it **has worked** there.	She / he / it **hasn't worked** there.

1 Work with a partner. Make true statements from the following cues.

Examples: I have lived in Boston.
I haven't lived in Madrid.

1. live
    a. in Los Angeles
    b. in Berlin
    c. in Hong Kong
    d. in Mexico City
    e. in Jakarta

2. study
    a. Spanish
    b. Math
    c. American History
    d. Chemistry
    e. Chinese

3. travel
    a. in Europe
    b. in Africa
    c. in Asia
    d. in Australia
    e. in South America

4. visit
    a. Mexico
    b. Egypt
    c. France
    d. Thailand
    e. Canada

2 Complete the following sentences with the past participle. Use the verbs in parentheses.

1. Technology has ___changed___ (change) our lives.
2. Technology has _____ (help) to make travel faster, easier, and cheaper.
3. Long-distance communication has _____ (become) faster and simpler.
4. Computers have _____ (open) new possibilities for communication.
5. Telephones have _____ (give) us a way "to stay in touch" with our friends and families from almost any place on earth.
6. Computer technology has _____ (bring) many improvements in our lives.
7. Hundreds of millions of people have _____ (use) the Internet to communicate.
8. All of this technology has _____ (make) our planet seem much smaller.

C. Present Perfect Tense: Questions

Yes / No Questions	Affirmative	Negative
Have I / you / we / they **helped**?	Yes, I / you / we / they **have**.	No, I / you / we / they **haven't**.
Has he / she / it **helped**?	Yes, he / she / it **has**.	No, he / she / it **hasn't**.

Information Questions	Possible Answers
Who has visited Russia? **Where has** she **lived**?	Nancy has been there twice. She has lived in five countries.

3   Talk about your experiences. In pairs, ask and answer these questions. Then, you can choose one question to answer in a short composition.

Example: What is the most unusual thing you have done during this course?

The most unusual thing I have done is scuba diving.

1. What is the most unusual thing you have done this year?
2. What is the hardest thing you have done?
3. Who is the funniest person you have met during this course?
4. What is the best movie you have seen?
5. What is the longest story or book you have read during this course?
6. What is the prettiest place you have visited this year?
7. What is the best food you have tried recently?
8. What is the most interesting thing that you have learned (besides English grammar, of course!)?
9. What is best song you have heard recently?
10. What is the most dangerous thing you have done?

D. The Passive Voice Versus the Active Voice

Many verbs in English can use either the active or the passive voice. Compare:

Active: John mailed the letter.

The active voice focuses on the person or thing that *does* the action: *John*.

Passive: The letter was mailed (by John).

The passive voice focuses on the person or thing that *receives* the action: *the letter*.

In some passive sentences, it is important to know who did the action. These sentences use *by* + person or thing. In other passive sentences, the result of the action is more important. These sentences do not use *by*. Compare:

Without *by*	With *by*
The letter was mailed.	The letter was mailed **by John, not by Sue**.
The book was written in 1999.	The book was written **by Mary Gill**.
The window was broken last week.	The window was broken **by three teenage boys in blue jeans**.

E. The Passive Voice with Simple Tenses

	Affirmative	**Negative**
Active Voice	John repaired the car.	Mary didn't fix the phones.
Passive Voice	Subject + *be* + past participle	Subject + *be* + *not* + past participle
Simple Past	The car **was repaired**.	The phones **weren't fixed**.
Simple Present	The car **is repaired**.	The phones **aren't fixed**.
Simple Future	The car **will be repaired**.	The phones **won't be fixed**.

4 Complete the following with the passive form of the verb. Use the simple past, present, or future tense. For a list of the irregular past participles, see Appendix 3, page 222.

Example: pay   The bill ___was paid___ yesterday.

Usually, the bills ___are paid___ at the beginning of the month.

That bill ___will be paid___ tomorrow.

1. finish   The project _____ yesterday.

Their project _____ now.

Gloria's project _____ next week.

2. elect   The next president _____ a month from now.

Jack _____ president of the club last month.

A new president _____ every year.

3. give   Jose _____ the prize last week.

Who _____ the prize next week?

Prizes _____ each week.

4. make   That decision _____ at last month's meeting.

In general, decisions _____ at the monthly meeting.

An important decision _____ tomorrow night.

5. not do   The work _____ tomorrow.

The work _____ on Fridays.

The work _____ last night.

6. not understand   His speech last night _____.

Esperanto _____ by most people.

Your perception _____ tomorrow. Please simplify it.

5 Complete the following story with the simple past tense. Choose the active or the passive voice. Use the verbs in parentheses.

Gandhi, A Model of Nonviolent Action

Mohandas K. Gandhi was one of the most important political activists of all time. He _was born_ (bear) in 1869, and he _____ (die) in 1948. He _____ (live) in Africa and India, but he _____ (know) worldwide for his work. He _____ (become) famous because he _____ (use) nonviolent action.

During Gandhi's life, India _____ (control) by Great Britain. Even though many Indians _____ (want) independence, they _____ (not give) control of their country by the British. Many different ideas _____ (discuss) about how to get independence. Some Indians _____ (buy) guns and _____ (fight) in bloody confrontations, but Gandhi _____ (teach) nonviolent action.

Finally, in 1947, India _____ (give) independence. Gandhi's work _____ (not finish) because the new India _____ (face) with many new problems. But, sadly, Gandhi _____ (kill) in 1948. Gandhi's work _____ (end) with his death, but his ideas and beliefs _____ (remain).

Video Activities: Recycling

Before You Watch.

1. What are these things usually made of? Write P for paper, A for aluminum, G for glass or PL for plastic. More than one answer may be correct.

   _____ soda cans   _____ magazines

   _____ shampoo bottles   _____ wine bottles

   _____ cereal box   _____ light bulb

2. What is the best way to get rid of trash?

   a. burn it   b. bury it   c. recycle it

Watch.

1. Edco is a company that _____.

   a. buys trash

   b. makes trash

   c. recycles trash

2. Check the kinds of trash that you see.

   _____ milk bottles   _____ newspapers

   _____ dishes   _____ clothes

   _____ bones   _____ cans

Watch Again.

Number the steps in the recycling process.

_____ Workers sort the trash into piles.

_____ Edco sends recycled material to customers.

_____ Workers collect the trash.

_____ Large trucks dump the trash at Edco.

After You Watch.

Write a paragraph about trash in your community. Think about these things. What do people do with their trash? Do they burn it? Do they bury it? Do they dump it on the land? What are some solutions to the problem of trash?

Appendices

Appendix 1

Parts of Speech

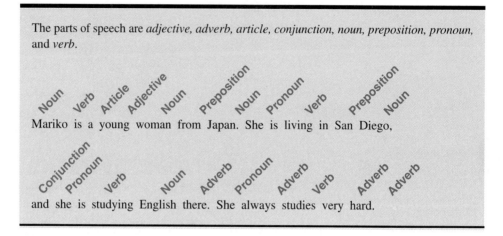

The parts of speech are *adjective, adverb, article, conjunction, noun, preposition, pronoun,* and *verb*.

| Noun | Verb | Article | Adjective | Noun | Preposition | Noun | Pronoun | Verb | Preposition | Noun |

Mariko is a young woman from Japan. She is living in San Diego,

| Conjunction | Pronoun | Verb | Noun | Adverb | Pronoun | Adverb | Verb | Adverb | Adverb |

and she is studying English there. She always studies very hard.

Sentence Parts / Word Order

Subject	Verb	Phrase	Subject	Verb	Object
Mariko	is	from Japan.	Mariko	studies	English.
Mariko	studies	every night.	She	always does	her homework.

Grammar Terms

Singular	= one	a boy	one dog
Plural	= two or more	boys	three dogs
Subject	= the main person, place, thing, or idea in a sentence.	**Mariko** came yesterday. **She** is from Japan. **Her mother** is going to visit her soon.	
Verb	= an action or situation	Mariko **came** yesterday. She **is** from Japan.	
Object	= the receiver of an action	Mariko met **her mother** at the airport. Mariko bought **a present** for her mother.	
Phrase	= two or more words together	yesterday afternoon from Japan in the United States	
Sentence	= a subject / verb combination that expresses a complete idea	Mariko came yesterday afternoon. She is from Japan. She is living in the United States. (*not:* She from Japan. 　　　She in the United States.)	

Appendix 2

Numbers

This chart gives you both the cardinal and the ordinal numbers. Note that the thirties, forties, and so on, follow the same pattern as the twenties.

Cardinal	Ordinal	Cardinal	Ordinal
zero		twenty	twentieth
one	first	twenty-one	twenty-first
two	second	twenty-two	twenty-second
three	third	twenty-three	twenty-third
four	fourth	twenty-four	twenty-fourth
five	fifth	twenty-five	twenty-fifth
six	sixth	twenty-six	twenty-sixth
seven	seventh	twenty-seven	twenty-seventh
eight	eighth	twenty-eight	twenty-eighth
nine	ninth	twenty-nine	twenty-ninth
ten	tenth	thirty	thirtieth
eleven	eleventh	forty	fortieth
twelve	twelfth	fifty	fiftieth
thirteen	thirteenth	sixty	sixtieth
fourteen	fourteenth	seventy	seventieth
fifteen	fifteenth	eighty	eightieth
sixteen	sixteenth	ninety	ninetieth
seventeen	seventeenth	(one) hundred	(one) hundredth
eighteen	eighteenth	(one) thousand	(one) thousandth
nineteen	nineteenth	(one) million	(one) millionth

Calendar Information

Days of the Week		Months of the Year		Seasons
Sunday	Sun.	January	Jan.	Winter
Monday	Mon.	February	Feb.	Spring
Tuesday	Tues.	March	Mar.	Summer
Wednesday	Wed.	April	Apr.	Autumn or Fall
Thursday	Thurs.	May		
Friday	Fri.	June		
Saturday	Sat.	July		
Sunday	Sun.	August	Aug.	
		September	Sept.	
		October	Oct.	
		November	Nov.	
		December	Dec.	

Appendix 3

Irregular Verbs

Simple Form	Past	Past Participle	Simple Form	Past	Past Participle
be	was / were	been	leave	left	left
bear	bore	born	lend	lent	lent
become	became	become	lose	lost	lost
begin	began	begun	make	made	made
bite	bit	bitten	mean	meant	meant
blow	blew	blown	meet	met	met
break	broke	broken	pay	paid	paid
bring	brought	brought	put	put	put
build	built	built	read	read	read
buy	bought	bought	ride	rode	ridden
catch	caught	caught	ring	rang	rung
choose	chose	chosen	run	run	run
come	came	come	say	said	said
cost	cost	cost	see	saw	seen
do	did	done	sell	sold	sold
draw	drew	drawn	send	sent	sent
drink	drank	drunk	shake	shook	shaken
drive	drove	driven	shoot	shot	shot
eat	ate	eaten	shut	shut	shut
fall	fell	fallen	sing	sang	sung
feed	fed	fed	sit	sat	sat
feel	felt	felt	sleep	slept	slept
fight	fought	fought	speak	spoke	spoken
find	found	found	spend	spent	spent
fly	flew	flown	stand	stood	stood
forget	forgot	forgotten	steal	stole	stolen
freeze	froze	frozen	sweep	swept	swept
get	got	gotten	swim	swam	swum
give	gave	given	take	took	taken
go	went	gone	teach	taught	taught
grow	grew	grown	tear	tore	torn
hang	hung	hung	tell	told	told
have	had	had	think	thought	thought
hear	heard	heard	throw	threw	thrown
hit	hit	hit	understand	understood	understood
hold	held	held	win	won	won
hurt	hurt	hurt	write	wrote	written
keep	kept	kept			
know	knew	known			

Appendix 4

Comparative and Superlative Forms of Adjectives and Adverbs

Rules	Positives	Comparatives	Superlatives
Add -er and -est to: one-syllable adjectives	nice young	nicer younger	the nicest the youngest
adjectives and adverbs that have the same form	early fast hard late	earlier faster harder later	the earliest the fastest the hardest the latest
Add -er and -est or use more, less, the most, the least with two-syllable adjectives	funny* shallow slender	funnier more funny shallower more shallow slenderer more slender	the funniest the most funny the shallowest the most shallow the slenderest the most slender
Use more, less, the most, the least with longer adjectives and most -ly adverbs	difficult interesting quickly slowly	more difficult more interesting more quickly more slowly	the most difficult the most interesting the most quickly the most slowly

* With words ending in -y, the -er and -est forms are more common, although both forms are used.

Irregular Adjectives and Adverbs

Adjectives	Adverbs	Comparatives	Superlatives
bad	badly	worse	the worst
good	—	better	the best
well	well	better	the best
far	far	farther	the farthest
—	—	further	the furthest
little	—	less	the least
many	—	more	the most
much	much	more	the most

Tapescript

Chapter 1   Neighborhoods, Cities, and Towns

PART 1   Listening to Conversations

2   Vocabulary Preview. Page 3. See student text.

3   Listening for Main Ideas. Page 3.

Ali:	Beth! Hey, Beth! How's it going?
Beth:	Ali! Hi! I'm fine. How're you?
Ali:	Fine, thanks. Beth, this is Lee. Lee, this is my friend, Beth.
Lee:	Nice to meet you.
Beth:	Nice to meet you too. Are you from around here?
Lee:	No, I'm from Seoul, Korea.
Beth:	Oh, that's interesting. Seoul's the capital of Korea, isn't it?
Lee:	Yes, that's right. How about you? What's your hometown?
Beth:	I'm from San Anselmo, California.
Lee:	Oh, really? Is that a big city?
Beth:	No, it's a small town in Northern California. There are about 20,000 people there. What's the population of Seoul?
Lee:	It's a really big city. There are over thirteen million people in Seoul.
Beth:	Wow! That's a lot of people!
Lee:	Yes, it is. But there's good public transportation, so it isn't bad.
Beth:	Uh-oh. I have to run. The library closes in ten minutes. See you guys later.
Lee:	Bye Beth.
Ali:	Take care, Beth.
Beth:	You too. Bye.

4   Listening for Specific Information. Page 3. Listen again. See text for Activity 3.

7   Listening for Stressed Words. Page 5. See student text.

8   Comparing Long Forms and Contractions. Page 5. See student text.

9   Listening for Contractions. Page 5.

1. I'm fine.
2. He's from Seoul.
3. It's the capital of Korea.
4. There are many people there.
5. What is the population?

Listening Skills

Getting Meaning from Context

1 Using Context Clues. Page 7.

Conversation 1

Beth: Alicia, this is my friend Jamie.
Alicia: Pleased to meet you.
Jamie: Nice to meet *you*. Are you from around here?
Alicia: No, I'm from Mexico.
Jamie: Where in Mexico—Mexico City?
Alicia: Uh-huh.
Jamie: So, what's the city like?
Alicia: It's huge. There're around twenty million people living there.

Question 1. What is Mexico City like?

Jamie: Wow! That's a really big city!
Alicia: Yeah, it sure is. I think it's the largest city in the world.

Conversation 2

Ali: So, Lee. Are you going home for New Year's?
Lee: Are you joking? Seoul's pretty far from here!
Ali: That's no problem. There're a lot of flights to Seoul from this city.
Lee: Yeah, but you're forgetting one important thing.
Ali: What's that?
Lee: The airfare! I'm a poor student, remember?

Question 2. Why isn't Lee going home for New Year's?

Ali: So, how much is it to Seoul?
Lee: Almost a thousand dollars! That's too much money for me!

Conversation 3

Man: Excuse me, driver. Does this bus go to Central Avenue?
Bus Driver: Yes, it's the second stop.
Man: So it's not very far?
Bus Driver: Nah! It's only about half a mile.
Man: Really! Well, it's a nice day today, and I'm not in a hurry. And if it's that close ... hmm . . .

Question 3. How will the man go to Central Avenue?

Bus Driver: C'mon, buddy! Are you getting on the bus or not?
Man: Sorry, driver. I'll just walk to Central Avenue. Thanks anyway.

Conversation 4

Beth: So, how do you get to the university every day?

Lee: I take the subway. It's really fast from my apartment. How 'bout you?

Beth: Yeah, the subway *is* fast . . . but I take the bus instead.

Lee: Why? It's so slow. . . .

Beth: Well, I can always get a seat. And there's room for all my books.

Question 4. Why doesn't Beth take the subway?

Lee: Yeah, I know what you mean. The subway is way too crowded . . .

Beth: Yeah, the bus is much more comfortable.

Conversation 5

Ali: Hey, Lee. How's it goin'?

Lee: Great. What's new with you?

Ali: I've got a new place to live.

Lee: Hey, that's great. What's it like?

Ali: Well, it's real old and it's pretty small . . . but the best thing is it's a five-minute walk to school!

Question 5. What does Ali like about his new place to live?

Lee: Wow, you're really close to school!

Ali: Yeah, that way, I can sleep longer in the morning!

Listening for Time and Distance

3 **Vocabulary Preview. Page 8.** See student text.

4 **Listening for Main Ideas. Page 8.**

Woman: So, how do you get to school every day?

Man: I take the subway. It's fast.

Woman: You don't take the bus?

Man: Nah, the bus's too slow. It takes 30 minutes to get to school from my place.

Woman: Yeah, I know what you mean.

Man: How 'bout you?

Woman: Oh, I walk — my apartment is close — about a mile from school. It's just a fifteen-minute walk.

Man: Wow, that's great. My place is far from school — about ten miles. So I *can't* walk . . .

Woman: Yeah, that's about a three-hour walk!

5 **Listening for Time and Distance. Page 8.** Listen again. See text for Activity 4.

Listening for Fares

8   Vocabulary Preview. Page 10. See student text.

9   Listening for the Main Idea. Page 10.

Public Transportation in Vancouver, Canada

There are many kinds of public transportation in Vancouver. There are buses, ferries, the Sky Train elevated railway, and the West Coast Express trains. The transportation system is divided into three zones. The fare for one zone is $1.50, and $2.25 for two or three zones. In the evening, on weekends, and on holidays, the fare is $1.50 for all zones. There are special fares for seniors, students, and children: $1.00 for one zone, $1.50 for two zones, and $2.00 for three zones. These fares are for the bus, the ferry, and the Sky Train. You need exact change for tickets on the bus. For the ferry and the Sky Train, you buy tickets in advance at machines at the station. To save money, buy a Day Pass. It's good for travel all day long on any form of transportation. A Day Pass costs $6.00 for adults and $4.00 for children.

10   Listening for Fares. Page 10. Listen again. See text for Activity 9.

Chapter 2   Shopping and e-Commerce

PART 1   ## Listening to Conversations

2   Vocabulary Preview. Page 28. See student text.

3   Listening for Main Ideas. Page 29.

Alicia:	Hi, Beth. Come on in . . .
Beth:	Hi, Alicia! How're you doing?
Alicia:	Pretty good.
Beth:	Alicia, this is my friend Ali. He's from Egypt.
Alicia:	Hi, Ali. Nice to meet you.
Ali:	Nice to meet you too.
Beth:	So, Alicia, we're going to go shopping. Do you want to come?
Alicia:	Gee, I dunno . . . I mostly do online shopping these days.
Ali:	Why?
Alicia:	Because it saves time.
Ali:	Yeah and I guess it saves energy, too.
Beth:	What do you mean?
Ali:	Well, you don't have to drive your car. . .
Alicia:	Right. And you don't have to look for parking, either. The mall is so crowded these days . . .
Beth:	Yeah, but you can't see things. And you can't touch them! I like old-fashioned shopping!
Ali:	Yeah, and it's such a nice day. . . why do you want to sit in front of a computer screen?
Alicia:	Yeah, I see what you mean . . . but with all this online shopping, I don't have much money left!

Beth: But you can come with us and *save* money.

Alicia: How?

Beth: We aren't going to take any money or credit cards with us. We aren't going to spend any money . . . we're going *window*-shopping.

Alicia: Great idea! Then I *am* going!

4 **Listening for Specific Information. Page 30.** Listen again. See text for Activity 3.

7 **Listening for Stressed Words. Page 31.** See student text.

8 **Comparing Long and Reduced Forms. Page 32.** See student text.

9 **Listening for Reductions. Page 32.** Reductions are marked with *.

1. It's nice to meet you.

2. Arencha* comin'*?

3. I'm spendin'* too much money.

4. Do you want to go shopping?

5. Do you hafta* study today?

PART 2   **Listening Skills**

Getting Meaning from Context

1 **Using Context Clues. Page 34.**

Part 1

Beth: Wow! This is a really big mall!

Alicia: Yeah, it is. Hey, I think I want to spend some money after all!

Ali: Well, maybe there's a bank here. . .

Beth: No, she doesn't need a bank. She can just use that machine over there.

Alicia: Oh, yeah. . . Let's see if I have my card. . .

Ali: How much are you gonna take out?

Alicia: Oh, maybe $200 . . .

Question 1. What are Ali, Alicia, and Beth talking about?

Ali: So, what's that called in English — a change machine?

Alicia: No, it's an automated teller, right?

Beth: Yeah. Or ATM for Automated Teller Machine.

Ali: Wait a minute, have you forgotten? We aren't going to need that. We're saving our money, right? Let's just keep window-shopping.

Part 2

Ali: Hey! Let's go in here! Look at all that great equipment!

Beth: Uh-oh, Alicia! Ali loves soccer and baseball. He's going to want to do more than window-shopping in this store.

Alicia: I think you're right. C'mon, Ali. You're not going in there, are you?

Question 2. What shop are Ali, Alicia, and Beth standing in front of now?

Ali: C'mon, just for a minute. I really love sports.

Alicia: Yes, but we are supposed to be window-shopping. Besides, mmm! Can you smell that?

Ali and Beth: Yeah!

Part 3

Beth: Fresh chocolate chip cookies!

Alicia: And brownies!

Ali: It all smells delicious. But we don't have any money, remember?

Alicia: Well, I do have about $4.00

Ali: OK, let's go!

Question 3. Where are they going now?

Beth: Wow! What a great bakery! I'll have one chocolate chip cookie.

Alicia: They're $1.50 each, three for $4.00. We have just enough.

Ali: Thanks, Alicia. Mmm!

Part 4

Ali: Where to now?

Beth: How about across the way? We can spend a few minutes looking at the new magazines and best sellers.

Alicia: Well, if you really want to. But I don't really like English magazines …

Ali: I'll bet they have Spanish magazines …

Question 4. Where are Ali and Beth going to go next?

Alicia: Nah, you two go to the bookstore. I'm going somewhere else.

Part 5

Beth: All right, Alicia. Then let's meet in front of the elevators in half an hour — at one o'clock, OK?

Alicia: OK. I'm going to look at some sweaters and boots. It's getting cold, you know.

Ali and Beth: OK.

Question 5. Where is Alicia going?

Alicia: Oh, Beth. Isn't there a good clothing store on the first floor?

Beth: Yes, there is. Go down those stairs and turn right.

Listening for Prices

3 **Vocabulary Preview. Page 34.** See student text.

4   **Listening for the Main Idea. Page 34.**

Ad 1
Are you looking for a great pair of jeans? How about Wild West jeans? Cost Club has Wild West blue jeans for only $29.99 a pair—the lowest price in town!!

Ad 2
Get the best price on Wild West blue jeans at Lowe's Discount House. Lowe's has your favorite jeans for only $31.99. That's right ... only $31.99! Hurry, before . . .

Ad 3
Morton's Department Store is having its Big Spring Sale! All your favorite brands are on sale now. Just listen to these prices: Wild West jeans for only $35.99! Spring Step . . .

5   **Listening for Store Names. Page 35.** Listen to the ads again. See text for Activity 4.

6   **Listening for Prices. Page 35.** Listen to the ads again. See text for Activity 4.

7   **Listening to Compare Prices. Page 35.** Listen to the ads again. See text for Activity 4.

Listening to Online Shopping Information

10   **Vocabulary Preview. Page 37.** See student text.

11   **Listening for the Main Idea. Page 37.**

SuperMall.com
Online shoppers now have a special place to buy everything they need: SuperMall.com. SuperMall.com is a shopping Website, but it's different from other online shopping sites. First of all, you can buy *anything* at SuperMall.com. No more going to one site for food, another for gifts, and another for furniture. SuperMall.com offers everything from groceries to clothes to refrigerators, all at one Website, and all in one transaction. And no more filling out several different online forms with your credit card and shipping information. Another big difference is that SuperMall.com promises to deliver your purchases *one hour* after you place your order. Now that's *really* saving time . . .

12   **Listening to Information about Online Shopping. Page 37.** Listen again. See text for Activity 11.

Chapter 3   Friends and Family

PART 1   Listening to Conversations

2   **Vocabulary Preview. Page 50.** See student text.

3 **Listening for the Main Idea. Page 51.**

Ali: Hi, Lee! Beth and I are going to see a movie. Come with us.
Lee: OK. Just a minute.
Beth: What are you reading, Lee?
Lee: A letter from my family.
Beth: But why are you so sad?
Lee: I miss them. I guess I'm homesick.
Ali: Yeah, I sometimes get homesick for my family.
Beth: Me, too. I really want to see my family and friends in California soon.
Ali: Do you usually get letters from your family, Lee?
Lee: Yes, two or three times a month. How about you?
Beth: I usually call home.
Ali: I usually stay in touch by e-mail because it's inexpensive.
Lee: Well, I really want to talk to my family. But it's expensive to call Korea.
Beth: Oh, call them, Lee! Just talk for three minutes.
Ali: Yeah, that's not very expensive. In fact, you can use my phone card.
Beth: Good idea! Call now before we go to the movies. There's pay phone over there.
Lee: You're right. I really need to talk to them. But wait for me, OK?
Beth: Great!
Ali: Sure.

4 **Listening for Specific Information. Page 51.** Listen again. See text for Activity 3.

7 **Listening for Stressed Words. Page 52.** See student text.

8 **Comparing Long and Reduced Forms. Page 53.** See student text.

9 **Listening for Reductions. Page 53.** Reductions are marked with *.

1. Are you gonna* come with us?
2. I don't miss them very much.
3. I can go to the movies with you.

4. What're you doing?
5. Beth 'n* I are studying.
6. Why're you sad?

| PART 2 | **Listening Skills** |

Getting Meaning from Context

1 **Using Context Clues. Page 54.**

Conversation 1

Beth: Where are you from, Lee?
Lee: I'm from Seoul, Korea.
Beth: I've been there. It's nice.
Lee: Yeah, I sure miss it!

Question 1. What is Lee homesick for?

Beth: It sounds like you're homesick for Seoul.
Lee: That's right! But I'm going to visit there next year.

Conversation 2

Ali: Hello?
Beth: Hello, Ali? This is Beth.
Ali: Hi, Beth. How are you doing?
Beth: Fine, thanks. Is David home?
Ali: No, he's skiing. He isn't coming back until tomorrow night.
Beth: Hmm. OK. Would you tell him I called?
Ali: Sure.
Beth: Also, would you ask him to call me when he gets back?
Ali: OK, Beth. I will.

Question 2. Who does Beth want to call her?

Ali: I'll have David call you tomorrow evening.
Beth: Thanks a lot, Ali. Bye.
Ali: Bye, Beth.

Conversation 3

Lee: Hi, Alicia! What are you doing?
Alicia: Hi, Lee. Oh, I'm looking at some pictures of my family.
Lee: Can I see them too?
Alicia: Of course. This is a picture of all of us. That's my mom and dad on the left.
Lee: Your mom's very pretty.
Alicia: Thanks . . . And that's my older brother next to Mom. My little sister is the one on the right. She's still in high school.

Question 3. How many children are in Alicia's family?

Lee: So your parents had three children?
Alicia: Uh-huh. I'm the middle child.

Conversation 4

Ali: Hey, listen to this: my little brother started school last week!
David: Great. What else does it say?
Ali: My cousin Nabil got a new job, and his wife just had a baby.
David: Gee, it's great to get news from home, isn't it?

Question 4. What's Ali doing?

Ali: Yeah. After reading this letter from my parents, I don't feel so homesick anymore.

Conversation 5

Beth: I'm going to call my family, Ali. Do you want to speak to them?
Ali: Sure, but . . . er . . . Beth, y' know, it's not 5 P.M., and it's a weekday.

Beth: So?

Ali: Well, the rates are high now. They go down after 5 o'clock. It's 4:40 now. Let's wait a few minutes.

Beth: Hmm.

Ali: And if you want cheaper rates, wait until tomorrow. The rates are lower on Saturday and Sunday.

Question 5. When can Beth get the cheapest rates?

Beth: All right. That's a good suggestion, Ali. I'll wait and call this weekend, on Saturday.

Listening to Voicemail Messages

3 Vocabulary Preview. Page 55. See student text.

4 Listening for the Main Idea. Page 55.

Outgoing [David]: Hello. This is David. I'm not in right now, but if you leave a message, I'll call you back as soon as I can.

Message 1: Hi, David. This is Amy. I'm sorry I couldn't meet you at school today. I'm sick. Call me back . . . I'll be home all night. The number is 555-4235. Bye.

Message 2: Hello. This is Beth. I'm calling to find out if you want to go out to dinner with me tonight. I want to go to that new Vietnamese restaurant, Cha Gio. Call me back at 555-1867, or meet me there at 7 o'clock.

Message 3: Hey, David. This is Ramez. I need to borrow that English book from you . . . remember, the book we talked about? I'll come by your apartment about 6 to pick it up. See you later.

Message 4: Hello, son. We're just calling to remind you that we're arriving tomorrow at 10:25. You'll meet us at the airport, right? We're really looking forward to seeing you. Your mother can't wait. See you tomorrow.

Message 5: David? This is Alicia. I forgot to ask you a question today. Can you take me to school tomorrow? My car is at the repair shop. I'll expect you at 7:30 tomorrow morning unless you call. My number is 555-7656. Thanks a lot. I really appreciate it. Bye.

5 Listening to Voicemail. Page 55. Listen again. See text from Activity 4.

Listening to Descriptions of People

8 Vocabulary Preview. Page 56. See student text.

9 Listening for the Main Idea. Page 56.

Beth: OK, Lee, my friend, Sue, will sell you her old answering machine.

Lee: Great! How can I get it?

Beth: She's at the apartment. You'll recognize her: she's tall and slim, and she has short blond hair.

10 Listening to Descriptions of People. Page 57. Listen again. See text for Activity 9.

Chapter 4 | Health Care

Listening to Conversations

2 Vocabulary Preview. Page 70. See student text.

3 Listening for the Main Idea. Page 71.

Receptionist:	Health Clinic. Can I help you?
Ali:	Yes. I think I have the flu. I feel awful.
Receptionist:	Would you like to make an appointment?
Ali:	Yes, I'd like to see a doctor.
Receptionist:	All right. Can you come in tomorrow afternoon at 1:00?
Ali:	Yes, I can come then. Oh! Should I bring any money?
Receptionist:	No—just your ID and insurance card.
Ali:	OK.
Receptionist:	Now, could I have your name and insurance number?
Ali:	Yes. My family name is Halal—H-A-L-A-L. My first name is Ali—A-L-I. And my insurance number is 000-481-624.
Receptionist:	OK. You're all set. Don't forget to bring your health insurance card when you come in tomorrow.
Ali:	OK.
Receptionist:	All right, we'll see you tomorrow at 1:00.
Ali:	Yes, thank you . . . thank you very much. Bye.
Receptionist:	Bye.

4 Listening for Specific Information. Page 71. Listen again. See text for Activity 3.

7 Listening for Stressed Words. Page 72. See student text.

8 Comparing Long and Reduced Forms. Page 72. See student text.

9 Listening for Reductions. Page 73. Reductions are marked with *.

1. I'd like to make an appointment.
2. Would you like to see Dr. Johnson at eleven?
3. Cudya* make it at one?
4. All right. We'll see ya* at one.

Listening Skills

Getting Meaning from Context

1 Vocabulary Preview. Page 74. See student text..

2 Using Context Clues. Page 74.

Call 1

Caller 1: Yes. I'd like to make an appointment.
Woman: What seems to be the problem?
Caller 1: I've got a really bad headache.
Woman: Did you take your temperature?
Caller 1: No, but I think I've got a fever. My head feels warm.
Woman: Hmm. Sounds like the flu. When can you come in?

Question 1. Who is the speaker probably calling?

Woman: Health clinic. May I help you?
Caller 1: Yes, I'd like to make an appointment.

Call 2

Caller 2: Hello. I'd like to report a stolen bicycle.
Woman: May I have your name, please?
Caller 2: The last name is Chavez, C-H-A-V-E-Z. First name, Maria, M-A-R-I-A.
Woman: Address?
Caller 2: One twenty-one High Street, Apartment 3B.
Woman: And where was the bike stolen from?
Caller 2: In front of my apartment building. It was there when I left it last night, but I didn't put a lock on it and. . .

Question 2. Who is the woman probably calling?

Woman: Police department. Officer Wyman speaking.
Caller 2: Hello. I'd like to report a stolen bicycle.

Call 3

Caller 3: Hi. My name's Beth Johnston. I'd like to make an appointment.
Man: All right, Beth. Is this for a checkup or a cleaning?
Caller 3: A checkup. I think I have a bad cavity. Half the side of my head hurts.
Man: Which tooth hurts?
Caller 3: One of the back ones.
Man: Let me see . . .We can see you this afternoon if you can come in at 4:30.

Question 3. Who is Beth probably calling?

Man: Dental clinic. This is Mr. Adams.
Caller 3: Hi. My name's Beth Johnston. I'd like to make an appointment.

Call 4

Caller 4: Please! You must help me! My apartment's on fire!
Woman: Please try to stay calm, ma'am. Where is the fire?
Caller 4: There's smoke everywhere . . . !
Woman: Excuse me . . are you out of the apartment?
Caller 4: Yes, I am! Please send help immediately!
Woman: Now, ma'am, stay calm. Where are you located?

Question 4. Who is the woman probably calling?

Woman:	Fire department.
Caller 4:	Please! You must help me! My apartment's on fire!

Call 5

Caller 5:	Yes, I'd like to make an appointment.
Man:	Have you ever been here before?
Caller 5:	No, but I'm a student, and all of a sudden, I can't see things on the board in the front of the classroom very well. . .
Man:	OK. It sounds like you need an exam.
Caller 5:	Great. I've been so worried. . .

Question 5. Who is the caller probably calling?

Man:	Eye clinic. This is Sean.
Caller 5:	Yes, I'd like to make an appointment.

Listening to Instructions

4 Vocabulary Preview. Page 74. See student text.

5 Listening for the Main Idea. Page 75.

Ali:	I feel like I have a very bad cold. I have a fever, I ache all over, and I cough and sneeze all the time.
Dr. Dirks:	You probably have the flu, or influenza. It's much more serious than a cold. You have to take care of yourself, or you could become very sick. You should stay in bed and rest as much as possible. You can take two aspirin, four times a day. That will help the fever and the aches and pains. Be sure to drink plenty of fluids. Fruit juice and hot tea are the best. Here's a prescription for some cough medicine. You can take it to any drugstore. Be sure to take your medicine with your meals because it might upset your stomach.
Ali:	I understand. Thanks.

6 Listening to Instructions. Page 75. Listen again. See text for Activity 5.

Listening to Complaints

9 Vocabulary Preview. Page 76. See student text.

10 Listening for Main Ideas. Page 76.

Speaker 1:	I have a terrible headache. The pain is right at the back of my head. It seems to go from ear to ear.
Speaker 2:	I think I have the flu. I vomited twice after breakfast this morning. I guess I shouldn't eat anything.
Speaker 3:	I was playing soccer and fell over another player. Now I can't stand up or walk. I think I broke my leg.
Speaker 4:	I just had a drink with ice, and now my tooth really hurts—here on the right side of my mouth. I must have a cavity.

Speaker 5: I tripped on the curb when crossing the street and twisted my ankle. I can walk, but it really hurts. I think I sprained it.

Speaker 6: I don't feel too bad, but I kept sneezing and coughing in class today. I knew there was a cold going around, but I didn't think I would catch it.

11 **Listening to Complaints. Page 76.** Listen again. See text for Activity 10.

Chapter 5   Men and Women

PART 1   Listening to Conversations

2   **Vocabulary Preview. Page 90.** See student text.

3   **Listening for the Main Idea. Page 91.**

Beth:	OK, great! I'll see you tomorrow at 7 o'clock. Right. Bye!
Alicia:	Hmm. Who was that?
Lee:	Yeah! Someone special?
Beth:	That was Michel, a really nice guy in my computer science class. He asked me out. I accepted, so . . .
Alicia:	So, one phone call, and now you have a boyfriend!
Beth:	Oh, c'mon, Alicia. He's not my boyfriend—yet!
Alicia:	Well, it sounds nice. In Mexico, I needed my parents' permission to go out on a date with a boy.
Lee:	Yeah . . . in Korea, a long time ago, parents used to arrange all dates—and marriages, too.
Beth:	Wow! That's strict!
Lee:	Yes, but arranged dates and marriages aren't very common in Korea now.
Alicia:	So, Lee, how about going out with a girlfriend of mine from my math class?
Lee:	Is she Korean?
Alicia:	No-o. Is that important?
Lee:	Not really, but my parents are a little strict. They might not like it.
Beth:	You mean your parents decide—even though you don't live with them?
Lee:	No-o. I just have to . . . .
Alicia:	You just have to get your parents' permission, right?
Lee:	Wrong! OK. I don't know why you want to be a cross-cultural matchmaker. But I'll go out with your friend.
Alicia:	Great! I'll call her so I can introduce you.

4   **Listening for Specific Information. Page 91.** Listen again. See text for Activity 3.

7   **Listening for Stressed Words. Page 92.** See student text.

8   **Comparing Long and Reduced Forms. Page 92.** See student text.

9   **Listening for Reductions. Page 93.** Reductions are marked with *.

1. What did you do last weekend?
2. Where ja* go on Sunday?
3. When ja* get up this morning?
4. How ja* get to school?
5. Who did you come to school with?
6. Why did you take the bus?

Getting Meaning from Context

1   Vocabulary Preview. Page 94. See student text.

2   Using Context Clues. Page 94.

Conversation 1

Alicia: So, Beth, how was your date with that guy in your computer science class ... what's his name?

Beth: Michel. We had a great time. Of course, on Friday night the Mann Theater is really crowded. We had to wait forty-five minutes to get our tickets.

Alicia: Yeah, it's terrible on the weekend. But you finally got in?

Beth: Uh-huh. And after the movie, we went to Mario's and had a pizza.

Question 1. What did Beth do on her date?

Alicia: So you went to a movie and a restaurant too, huh? That sounds nice . . .!

Conversation 2

Jennifer: What happened to you? Do you know what time it is?

Rob: Jennifer, please try to understand. I tried to get here by 1 o'clock, but the traffic was terrible!

Jennifer: Rob, it's almost 2:30. The traffic couldn't be that bad.

Rob: I'm really sorry. It won't happen again.

Question 2. Why is Jennifer upset?

Jennifer: Well, all right. But next time, call me if you're going to be late, OK?

Conversation 3

Dina: Hello?

Ali: May I speak to Dina, please?

Dina: This is Dina.

Ali: Hi, Dina. This is Ali.

Dina: Who?

Ali: Ali ... from your chemistry class.

Dina: Oh, hi, Ali. What's up?

Ali: I called to see if you wanted to go with me to a movie. There's a good one at the Mann Theater this Friday night.

Dina: Oh, thanks, Ali, but I'm already doing something this Friday night.

Question 3. What is Dina probably going to do?

Ali: Well, are you busy on Saturday? We can get a pizza or something. . .

Dina: Thanks, Ali, but I can't go out with you. I already have a boyfriend.

Conversation 4

Pat: Hello?

Ali: May I speak to Pat, please?

Pat: Speaking.

Ali: Hi, Pat. This is Ali from your English class.

Pat: Oh, hi, Ali. How're you doing?

Ali: Fine, thanks. Look, Pat, would you like to go to a movie with me on Friday night?

Pat: Gee, I'd like to, Ali, but I'm already doing something on Friday.

Question 4. What is Pat probably going to do?

Ali: Oh, well. Maybe some other time.

Pat: Hey, I'm not doing anything on Saturday. How 'bout going to the concert in the park that evening?

Ali: Great idea! I'll pick you up at 7 o'clock.

Conversation 5

Susan: Say, Lee. Do you want to go to the concert on Saturday?

Lee: Uh, yeah, sure. It's free, isn't it?

Susan: No, actually student tickets are $10 or $15 each, I think.

Lee: Hmm. Look, Susan, I'd like to go to the concert, but I don't think I can. . .

Question 5. Why can't Lee go to the concert?

Susan: Why can't you go?

Lee: Gee, I just don't think I have enough money to pay for you *and* me.

Susan: That's OK. I'm inviting you, so I'll pay.

Listening to Invitations

5 Vocabulary Preview. Page 95. See student text.

6 Listening for Main Ideas. Page 95.

Michel: Hello?

Beth: Hi, Michel. This is Beth. How are you?

Michel: Fine. How're you doing?

Beth: Great! I'm just calling to invite you over tomorrow night. My roommate and I are having a few people over for dinner. We might rent a movie. Can you come?

Michel: Sure, I'd love to. What time?

Beth: About 7 o'clock. It's going to be very informal.

Michel: Should I bring anything?

Beth: No, we have everything we need.

Michel: OK. Then I'll see you tomorrow about 7 o'clock.

Beth: Great! See you then.

7 Listening to Invitations. Page 95. Listen again. See text for Activity 6.

Listening to Responses

10   Vocabulary Preview. Page 97. See student text.

11   Listening for Main Ideas. Page 97.

> *David:*   Hey, there's a basketball game on Friday night!
> *Ali:*   So?
> *Beth:*   Who's playing?
> *David:*   The Seals and the Bears.
> *Beth:*   That sounds exciting!
> *David:*   So, do you want to go with me?
> *Ali:*   Uh-h-h, gee, David, maybe some other time.
> *David:*   How about you, Beth?
> *Beth:*   I'd love to! I'll meet you at 6 o'clock.

12   Listening to Responses. Page 97. Listen again. See text for Activity 11.

Chapter 6   Sleep and Dreams

PART 1   ## Listening to Conversations

2   Vocabulary Preview. Page 112. See student text.

3   Listening for Main Ideas. Page 113.

> *Beth:*   Ali! What's the matter? Can't you wake up this morning?
> *Ali:*   I was up late last night. My friend had a party. I only slept about four hours.
> *Alicia:*   Why didn't you stay in bed this morning?
> *Ali:*   I have to meet my study group at the library. We have a big test next week.
> *Beth:*   A big test? Why didn't you study last night instead of partying?
> *Ali:*   Oh, it's OK. I studied a lot before the party.
> *Alicia:*   Maybe that's not a good idea.
> *Ali:*   Why not?
> *Alicia:*   I read a research study. It said that if you don't get enough sleep after you study, you may forget 30% of what you studied! Especially if you studied something very complex.
> *Ali:*   30%? That's almost one-third!
> *Beth:*   Yes, that's a lot. Are you sure, Alicia?
> *Alicia:*   Yes. Even two days after you study— if you don't get enough sleep, you forget a lot. It's called being "sleep deprived".
> *Beth:*   Well, I read that eating right can help you study.
> *Ali:*   What you eat helps you study?
> *Beth:*   Yes, there are chemicals that help you stay alert. I think the best foods are fish, eggs, soy, rice, and peanuts.
> *Alicia:*   Where are you going, Ali?
> *Ali:*   Home to take a nap!

4 Listening for Specific Information. Page 113. Listen again. See text for Activity 3.

6 Listening for Stressed Words. Page 114. See student text.

7 Pronouncing Teens and Tens. Page 115. See student text.

8 Distinguishing between Teens and Tens. Page 115.

1. He is <u>14</u> years old.
2. I bought <u>thirteen</u> new books.
3. The price is <u>70</u> dollars.

4. It happened in <u>1980</u>.
5. We stayed for <u>15</u> days.
6. I live at 60 New Hope Road.

PART 2 # Listening Skills

Getting Meaning from Context

1 Using Context Clues. Page 117.

Part 1

Good morning, class. I hope you all had enough sleep last night (sound of laughter). If you read the chapter, you know that the topic for today is Sleep and the Human Brain. First, I will review the importance of sleep. Then I will tell you about some new research on sleep and studying. Finally, I will discuss the health benefits of sleep.

Question 1. What are you listening to: a conversation, a telephone call, or a lecture in a classroom?

This lecture will cover some of the information in your textbook and add some new information.

Part 2

We don't know why the human brain needs sleep. We do know that sleep is important for physical health and mental health. Your body needs sleep to stay healthy and strong. Your brain seems to need sleep for the same reason.

Question 2. What does sleep do for your brain?

Sleep helps your brain stay healthy. It helps you think clearly and remember more.

Part 3

Carlyle Smith, a psychology professor in Canada, did some research on sleep. He studied how sleep affects memory. He started by teaching students two things: first, a list of words and second, a difficult problem.

Question 3. Why did Carlyle Smith teach the students a list of words and a difficult problem?

Then Smith tested the students to see how much they remembered of the list of words and the problem.

Part 4

Before he gave the students the test, he had the students sleep different amounts for the next three nights. Some students slept 8 hours every night. Some students slept only 4 or 5 hours the first night; then they slept 8 hours the next two nights. Some students slept 8 hours the first night, only 4–5 hours the second night, and 8 hours the third night. Some students slept 8 hours the first night and the second night, but only 4–5 hours the third night.

Question 4. Why did Smith have the students sleep different amounts on the first, second and third nights?

Smith wanted to see if sleeping only a few hours for three nights after learning something new affects the memory.

Part 5

The results of the research showed that people remember better when they get enough sleep. Of course, the students who slept 8 hours every night did the best on the test. They remembered the list of words and the difficult problem very well. Students who slept only 4 or 5 hours the second night after learning the words and the problem also did very well. But the results were very different for the students who slept only 4 or 5 hours on the first night <u>or</u> the third night. They remembered the list of words just as well as the students who slept. Their test scores were the same on that test.

Question 5. How did the students who didn't sleep much on the first or third nights remember the difficult problem?

But the students who didn't sleep much on the first and third nights did not do well on the test on the difficult problem. They couldn't remember how to solve the problem. Smith concluded that it is very important to sleep enough the night after you learn something new <u>and</u> the third night after — but it might be safe to stay up late on the second night!

Listening to a Lecture

3 Vocabulary Preview. Page 118. See student text.

4 Listening for Main Ideas. Page 118.

Carlyle Smith's study on memory and sleep showed some interesting results. There were four subject groups in the study. All of the students learned a list of words and how to solve a complex problem. The first group of students slept 8 hours a night for three nights after learning the new material. One week later, they took a test on the words and the problem. They remembered all the material. Most scored 100% on both tests — on the list of words and the complex problem.

The second subject group only slept 4 or 5 hours the night after learning the material — they were sleep-deprived the first night. One week later, they still remembered the list of words, but they didn't remember how to solve the complex problem. Most scored 100% on the list of words, but only 70% on the complex problem.

The third subject group was sleep-deprived the second night after learning the new material. Strangely, they scored just as well as the first group —most answered 98% of the questions correctly on both tests — the list of words and the complex problem.

The fourth group slept well the first and second night, but they were sleep-deprived on the third night. This group had the same memory problems as the group that was sleep-deprived on the first night. They remembered the list of words, but not how to solve the problem. Their scores on the tests were the same as group 2.

5 Listening for Test Scores. Page 118. Listen again. See text for Activity 4.

Listening to a Dream

8 Vocabulary Preview. Page 120. See student text.

9 Listening for Main Ideas. Page 120.

I had the strangest dream last night! I was going to the movies with Beth. I went to her house to get her. But I wasn't wearing normal clothes; I was wearing a bathing suit and diving gear. Beth said, "Ali, take off that mask! I can't see your face." I tried to take the mask off, but my arms couldn't move! I had trouble getting on the bus because of the flippers on my feet. All the people were looking at us. Beth was so embarrassed! I wanted to take the mask off, but couldn't. At the theater, Beth had to pay for the tickets because my arms still wouldn't move. But when we went inside, everyone was wearing a mask! They all looked at Beth because she didn't have a mask on. Then she was even more embarrassed!

10 Listening to a Dream. Page 121. Listen again. See text for Activity 9.

Chapter 7   Work and Lifestyles

PART 1   Listening to Conversations

2 Vocabulary Preview. Page 136. See student text.

3 Listening for the Main Ideal. Page 137.

Alicia: What are you looking for, Ali?
Ali: I'm hoping to find a summer job in my major, public health.
Alicia: I'm sure you can. Do you have any experience in public health?
Ali: Yes, I do. I worked part-time in a lab in Egypt last summer.
Alicia: That's great. I want to find a job writing for a local newspaper. I'd like to be a reporter.
Ali: Your major's journalism, isn't it?
Alicia: Uh-huh. I had a great job last summer when I was in Mexico City.
Ali: Really? What did you do?
Alicia: I worked part-time for *Excelsior*. It's the biggest newspaper in Mexico.
Ali: What did you do there?

Alicia:	I wrote local news stories— you know, news about Mexico City. But someday I want to write international news stories. Then I can travel around the world and find out what people are like in other places.
Ali:	That sounds wonderful. I'm sure you can do it.
Alicia:	Are there any good jobs in public health on the bulletin board?
Ali:	No, I don't see anything interesting.
Alicia:	You should try looking on the Web. There are some great job sites. That's how I found the job in Mexico City.
Ali:	That's a good idea. Do I search for "public health"?
Alicia:	Try "jobs in public health" or the names of specific jobs. I searched for "newspaper reporter".
Ali:	I'll go to the computer lab right now and try that! See you later.

4   **Listening for Specific Information. Page 137.** Listen again. See text for Activity 3.

7   **Listening for Stressed Words. Page 139.** See student text.

8   **Pronouncing Majors and Job Titles. Page 139.** See student text.

9   **Distinguishing between Majors and Job Titles. Page 139.**

1. Henry is a journalism major at Columbia University.
2. The studies of an economist are important for people in business and government.
3. Do you like to read the reports of psychology research?
4. The company needs an accountant for its financial records.
5. Without biologists, we would not know much about plants and animals.
6. The study of the natural world and its laws is the focus of physics.
7. In the future, we will need a lot of technologists.

PART 2   # Listening Skills

Getting Meaning from Context

1   **Vocabulary Preview. Page 141.** See student text.

2   **Using Context Clues. Page 141.**

Conversation 1

Interviewer:	Come in!
Alicia:	Excuse me. May I see you now? I have an appointment.
Interviewer:	Of course. You're ... Alicia?
Alicia:	Yes, that's right. Alicia Morales.
Interviewer:	And you're interested in working for us?
Alicia:	Yes. I have some experience. I was a part-time reporter last summer for *Excelsior*.

| Interviewer: | I see. Well, this example of your writing is excellent. |

Question 1. Who is Alicia talking to?

| Interviewer: | As job interviewer for our newspaper, I think we might have an opening in the international news department. |
| Alicia: | Oh, I hope so! I would love to work on international stories! |

Conversation 2

David:	What are you going to do this summer, Lee? Going back to Korea?
Lee:	I'd like to, David, but I have to think about my future.
David:	Your future? What do you mean?
Lee:	Well, someday I want to help sick people. So I want to get some hospital experience.
David:	You mean working part-time in one?
Lee:	Uh-huh.

Question 2. What does Lee want to do this summer?

| David: | If you want to work in a hospital, you should visit County General Hospital. They may have part-time summer jobs. |
| Lee: | I will. Thanks. |

Conversation 3

Lee:	So how about you, David? What are your summer plans?
David:	I'm still not sure what I'm going to do. I should study, but my friend Bill — y' know, the one in San Francisco?
Lee:	Oh, right.
David:	He wants me to go with him to Europe in July and August.
Lee:	Really?
David:	Yeah. I'm thinking about it.

Question 3. What is David thinking about doing this summer?

| Lee: | That's a great plan. You *should* go to Europe this summer. |

Conversation 4

David:	Yes, but I have to think about September.
Lee:	Aren't you going to go back to school?
David:	Well, I *should* go back. But I'm getting tired of school. I want more experience in the real world.
Lee:	So you want more job experience?
David:	Uh-huh.

Question 4. What does David want to do in the fall?

| Lee: | I know how you feel. I want to work too, but I have to get out of school first. |

Conversation 5

| David: | Is that because you're an international student? |
| Lee: | That's right. I can only study with my student visa, except in the summer. Then I can work part-time. |

Question 5. Can Lee work?

> David: So you can work only in the summer? That's rough.
> Lee: Oh, it's not bad. But I have to be careful with money!

Listening to Job Interviews

4 Vocabulary Preview. Page 142. See student text.

5 Listening for Main Ideas. Page 142.

> Mrs. Kline: Rafael, your résumé is very impressive. Please tell me why you're interested in this job.
> Rafael: Well, I like working with computers, and the job sounds very challenging.
> Mrs. Kline: I see. Why should I give you a job with this company?
> Rafael: My work is accurate, and I learn quickly. In fact, I really like learning new information and new skills!
> Mrs. Kline: Good. You'll have a lot to learn here. Tell me, Rafael, what do you think you'll be doing in ten years?
> Rafael: I like working with people, so I'd like to be a department manager in ten years.

6 Listening to Job Interviews. Page 142. Listen again. See text for Activity 5.

Listening to Future Plans

9 Vocabulary Preview. Page 143. See student text.

10 Listening for the Main Idea. Page 143.

> Father: So what are your plans for this summer, David?
> David: Well, I could work for that construction company again. But I have a great opportunity to do some traveling and learn more about the world.
> Father: What's that?
> David: My friend, Bill, is going to travel around Europe this summer — he has some relatives in France he wants to visit, and he plans to go to Germany, Lithuania, and Latvia. He'll have a rental car, so all I need to pay for is my airfare and meals.
> Father: What about hotels when you're not staying with Bill's relatives?
> David: We'll stay in youth hostels. They're really cheap. I have enough money saved from my part-time job.
> Father: What about money for next year? For your books and other expenses?
> David: Well, I'll need to borrow a little from you. But this is a once in a lifetime chance— I really think I could learn a lot — and I can improve my French, too!

11 Listening to Future Plans. Page 144. Listen again. See text for Activity 10.

Chapter 8 Food and Nutrition

Listening to Conversations

---

2 Vocabulary Preview. Page 158. See student text.

3 Listening for the Main Idea. Page 159.

Meryl: What are you going to have, David?
David: I'm hungry! I want a double cheeseburger and a large order of fries.
Pat: Ugh! How many cheeseburgers do you eat every week? You had a couple at the picnic yesterday, didn't you?
David: Yeah,. . . so *what?* I *like* cheeseburgers!
Meryl: I think Pat's worried about you.
David: Why? I'm healthy!
Pat: But cheeseburgers have a lot of fat.
Meryl: And a lot of calories.
David: OK, OK! What are *you* going to have?
Pat: I'm going to have some tofu and rice.
David: Oh, I forgot. You're a vegetarian, right?
Pat: Right.
Meryl: Hmm. I think I'm going to have a salad.
David: Are you on a diet?
Meryl: No diet — I just like to eat healthy food.
David: What are you going to have to drink?
Pat: A large soda.
David: A large *soda?* But there's lots of sugar in soda!
Meryl: David's right, Pat. And sugar's bad for your teeth.
Pat: All right! I'll have a *diet* soda. There's no sugar in that!
David: Great! And I'll have a *salad* too.

4 Listening for Specific Information. Page 159. Listen again. See text for Activity 3.

7 Listening for Stressed Words. Page 160. See student text.

8 Comparing Long and Reduced Forms. Page 160. See student text.

9 Listening for Reductions. Page 161. Reductions are marked with *.

1. What are you going to have?
2. I think I'm gonna* have some tofu and rice.
3. We'd like a coupla* salads.
4. Isn't there a lot of fat in cheeseburgers?
5. They don't wanna* eat lotsa* fatty food.

Listening Skills

Getting Meaning from Context

1   Vocabulary Preview. **Page 162.** See student text.

2   Using Context Clues. **Page 162.**

Conversation 1

Lee: Everything looks delicious! What are you going to have?
Alicia: David says the onion soup here tastes great. I think that's what I'll have.
Lee: That sounds good.

Question 1. Where are Lee and Alicia?

Lee: Y'know, it's really nice to eat in a restaurant.
Alicia: It sure is.

Conversation 2

Alicia: No, thank you. Everything was delicious.
Lee: Yes, it was. But, waiter?
Waiter: Yes, sir?
Lee: What's this charge for?
Waiter: Hmm. Let me see. Oh, yes. That's for your drinks. One hot tea, 85 cents, and one cola, 80 cents.

Question 2. What's Lee talking about?

Lee: Oh, I see. Thanks for explaining the bill.
Waiter: You're welcome, sir.

Conversation 3

Beth: Now, David. What's next?
David: Hmm. Just a minute. Ah, . . . one cup of milk.
Beth: A cup of milk.
David: One teaspoon of salt.
Beth: A teaspoon of salt.
David: And one egg.
Beth: Right.
David: Beat the milk, salt, and egg mixture thoroughly and . . .

Question 3. What are David and Beth doing?

David: This is fun, isn't it?
Beth: Yes, it is. I really enjoy cooking.
David: But eating is even better!

Conversation 4

Ali:	Wow! This place is really big!
Alicia:	It *is* big, isn't it?
Ali:	Look at all this food!
Alicia:	Here's what we need for the salad. What's on the list?
Ali:	Let's see — lettuce, tomatoes, carrots, and cucumbers.

Question 4. Where are Ali and Alicia?

Ali:	All these fruits and vegetables look so fresh!
Alicia:	Yeah. These big supermarkets have good produce!

Conversation 5

Ali:	So, do we have everything on the shopping list?
Alicia:	I think so. Oh! We need spaghetti sauce. It's over there.
Ali:	Here it is. What kind should we buy?
Alicia:	Hmm. Here's one . . . spaghetti sauce with mushrooms . . . eight ounces, $1.06.
Ali:	That looks good. But here's another kind. It's only 99 cents.
Alicia:	Really? Let me see the label . . . spaghetti sauce with mushrooms . . . oh, but look *here*, Ali. There's only *six* ounces in this one.

Question 5. Which spaghetti sauce is the best buy?

Ali:	Oh, yeah, you're right. The eight-ounce size for $1.06 is the best buy. Let's buy that one.

Listening to Instructions

4   **Vocabulary Preview. Page 163.** See student text.

Noun	Verbs	Adverb
cheese grater	to chop	thoroughly
	to grate	
	to brown	

5   **Listening for Main Ideas. Page 163.**

Ali:	Beth, Alicia — I'm so happy to see you! I need some help.
Beth:	What's the problem, Ali?
Ali:	Well, you know I never cooked before I came to the university.
Alicia:	Uh-huh.
Ali:	I asked my mother for some recipes so I can make my favorite dishes. She sent me these, but I don't understand the instructions.
Beth:	We can try to help. What are the instructions you don't understand?
Ali:	First it says to "chop" some onions. My dictionary says "chop" means to cut. Do I cut the onions with scissors?
Alicia:	No. Chop just means to cut them up into very small pieces with a knife.
Ali:	Oh, OK. I get it. Now this one says to "brown" the onions.
Beth:	That means to cook it in a little oil until it turns brown all over.
Ali:	I've never seen "brown" as a verb before! This one — "mix thoroughly" I understand. It means to mix the things together completely, right?

Beth: Right.
Ali: What about this — "grate" the cheese? How do I grate cheese?
Alicia: You need a special tool for that — a cheese grater. It has little holes and sharp
          points on it. So that when you rub the cheese over it, thin bits of cheese fall through
          the holes. Then you can put the cheese on top of other foods like pizza. I have a
          cheese grater you can borrow.
Ali: Great! Thanks a lot. I'll invite you for dinner when I finish!

6 **Listening to Instructions. Page 163.** Listen again. See text for Activity 5.

Following Recipes

10 **Listening for the Main Idea. Page 165.**

Hi. I'm Wally Chan. Welcome to "Chan Can Cook." Today I'm making chili. You make
chili with beans, beef, and tomatoes.

First, chop an onion. Cut it into small pieces. Then, brown the onion and some ground
beef in a little oil. Cook the onion and beef in the oil until the onion is a little brown, and the
beef is all brown. Now, add the tomatoes and chili powder to the beef and onion. Chili powder
is hot, so just use a little if you don't like spicy food. Cook this mixture for about an hour,
stirring occasionally.

OK. Here's what it looks like when it's done. I like to serve the chili in a bowl with some
shredded cheese on top. Enjoy!

11 **Ordering Steps in a Recipe. Page 166.** Listen again. See text for Activity 10.

12 **Discussing Opinions about Food. Page 166.**

1. I like onions on my hamburgers.
2. Chili powder makes food too hot and spicy.
3. I eat a lot of cheese — with crackers, bread, and other foods.
4. Tomatoes are best in salad, with lettuce, oil, and vinegar.
5. I like beans when they are cooked with onions and garlic.
6. Cooking with oil can make you fat.
7. The best pizza has just tomato sauce and lots of cheese.
8. Foods like beans, rice, and potatoes should be eaten at every meal.
9. Onions are good cooked and uncooked.
10. I like a lot of pepper in my food.

Chapter 9 | Great Destinations

PART 1 | Listening to Conversations

2 Vocabulary Preview. Page 178. See student text.

3 Listening for Main Ideas. Page 179.

Beth:	What a great day to be out driving. These cherry blossoms are beautiful!
Ali:	Yes, I think I like Kyoto even more than that place we visited last summer — the Grand Canyon.
David:	The Grand Canyon was very different — you know, rugged and wild. This is so peaceful.
Ali:	Well, Japan is a very old country with a long history and many traditions.
Beth:	Yes — the western part of the United States is fairly new. That's why the mountains are so tall and the scenery is so rugged.
David:	It's cool to see so many different places. Uh-oh!
Beth:	David! What's wrong with the car?
Ali:	Yeah! Why are we going slower?
David:	Oh, *no*! I think we have a flat tire!
Beth:	We have a spare tire, don't we?
David:	Yes, I think so. I'll pull over.
David:	There it is. It *is* a flat tire. Now, who can help me change it?
Beth & Ali:	I can!
Beth:	It's too bad we have a flat tire.
Ali:	Yes, but at least we can take some photographs of the scenery now!

4 Listening for Specific Information. Page 179. Listen again. See text for Activity 3.

6 Listening for Stressed Words. Page 181. See student text.

7 Stress and Word Families. Pages 181–182. See student text.

PART 2 | Listening Skills

Getting Meaning from Context

1 Vocabulary Preview. Page 183. See student text.

2 Using Context Clues. Page 183.

Part 1

Beth:	Well, we've got everything in the trunk.
David:	I thought the tent wasn't going to fit!
Ali:	The sleeping bags and fishing equipment take up a lot of space, too.
Beth:	You guys have too much luggage, too.

Question 1. What did Beth, David, and Ali finish doing?

Beth: We just got everything in the car, and it's already almost lunchtime!

Part 2

David: Yes, so let's go find something to eat.
Beth: Where? There's not a town or restaurant anywhere *near* here.
Ali: Yes, there is. Look at this map. There's a town about five miles from here.
David: You're right! Let's go!

Question 2. What are Ali, David, and Beth going to do?

Beth: I'm so glad there's a town near here. It must have a restaurant or two. I'm really hungry!

Part 3

Ali: Well, that was a great lunch.
Beth: Yeah, we were lucky to find such a good restaurant way out here.
David: Thanks to you and your map!
Ali: Aww, it was easy. Say, why is it so dark outside?
Beth: *Look* at that sky! I don't like this. It's really cloudy.
David: You're right. I'll turn on the radio.

Question 3. Why is David going to turn on the radio?

Ali: See if you can find a weather report.

Part 4

Radio: . . . . and in southern New Mexico, there's a flash flood advisory through this evening with a 50 percent chance of rain this afternoon, increasing to 70 percent tonight. Lows expected tonight near freezing.

Question 4. What's the weather probably going to be like tonight?

Beth: Did you hear *that?* It's going to be really rainy and cold tonight.

Part 5

Ali: Maybe this is the night for us to stay in a motel.
David: I think so too. Camping's fun but not in the rain. Ah! We're almost in the town. Let's see if there's a motel.
Beth: David! Why didn't you stop?
Ali: Yeah! Didn't you see the sign? You could get a ticket!
David: No, I didn't! Sorry, guys!

Question 5. Why is David sorry?

Beth: Whew! Be *careful,* David!
David: You're right. I didn't even *see* that stop sign.

Listening to a Tour Guide

5   **Listening for Main Ideas. Page 185.**

Tour guide: This is the capitol building for the state of Georgia. The capitol building is famous. It has a gold roof. The gold came from the mountains of Georgia.

    Just east of the capitol building, in downtown Atlanta, is the Martin Luther King Jr. National Historic Site. It's a memorial to the great leader of the American Civil Rights Movement, Martin Luther King Jr. Martin Luther King Jr. was from Atlanta. His grave is at this site.

    Now, we're just east of the city of Atlanta. This is Stone Mountain. It's a natural hill of stone. It's famous because a man carved a picture of three Civil War generals on the side of the mountain. These generals are Jefferson Davis, Robert E. Lee, and Stonewall Jackson.

    Now, we're coming around to Interstate Highway I-20, to the west side of the city. This is Six Flags Amusement Park. It's a large amusement park with lots of roller coasters and other rides.

6   **Listening for Places on a Map. Page 185.** Listen again.

Number 1

Tour guide: This is the capitol building for the state of Georgia. The capitol building is famous. It has a gold roof. The gold came from the mountains of Georgia.

Number 2

Tour guide: Just east of the capitol building, in downtown Atlanta, is the Martin Luther King Jr. National Historic Site. It's a memorial to the great leader of the American Civil Rights Movement, Martin Luther King Jr. Martin Luther King Jr. was from Atlanta. His grave is at this site.

Number 3

Tour guide: Now, we're just east of the city of Atlanta. This is Stone Mountain. It's a natural hill of stone. It's famous because a man carved a picture of three Civil War generals on the side of the mountain. These generals are Jefferson Davis, Robert E. Lee, and Stonewall Jackson.

Number 4

Tour guide: Now, we're coming around to Interstate Highway I-20, to the west side of the city. This is Six Flags Amusement Park. It's a large amusement park with lots of roller coasters and other rides.

7   **Listening to a Tour Guide. Page 185.** Listen again. See text for Activity 6.

Listening for Flight Information

9   **Vocabulary Preview. Page 186.** See student text.

10   **Listening for the Main Idea. Page 186.**

    Travel agent: Yes, what can I do for you?

        Alicia: I'd like to go to Disney World, so I need information on flights to Florida.

Travel agent:	OK. I think I can get a good fare for you to Orlando, Florida. Do you want to go first class, business class, or coach?
Alicia:	Oh, coach, of course. I'd like the lowest fare you can find.
Travel agent:	All right. And that's one way or round trip?
Alicia:	Round trip. I'd like to leave on Sunday the 12th and return on Saturday the 18th.
Travel agent:	Well, there's a very low fare on Sunday morning. It's only $345, but it's not direct. You have to change planes in Chicago. There's a direct, nonstop flight, but the fare on that one is $680.
Alicia:	That's OK. I'll change planes in Chicago.
Travel agent:	OK. That's flight 690. It departs at 8:15 a.m. on Sunday the 12th and arrives in Orlando at 12:15.
Alicia:	That sounds good.
Travel agent:	Oh, there's one more thing. It's a special low fare, so the ticket is nonrefundable.
Alicia:	That's all right. I'm not going to change my plans.

11 **Listening for Flight Information. Page 187.** Listen again. See text for Activity 10.

Chapter 10 Our Planet

PART 1 Listening to Conversations

2 Vocabulary Preview. Page 200. See student text.

3 Listening for Main Ideas. Page 201.

Alicia:	Come in!
Lee:	Hi, Alicia. What are you doing?
Alicia:	Hi, Lee. I'm making a sign for Earth Day.
Lee:	*Earth* Day? What's that?
Alicia:	On Earth Day, people think about pollution and other problems with the environment.
Lee:	Really! When is Earth Day?
Alicia:	Next Monday.
Lee:	I've never heard of Earth Day. When did it start?
Alicia:	The first Earth Day was on April 22, 1970. A U.S. senator and a college student started it. They wanted people to be more aware of problems with the environment.
Lee:	What happens on Earth Day?
Alicia:	Well, one year, thousands of people marched in Washington D.C. to ask the U.S. government for laws on clean energy. In Italy, 150 towns and cities had Car-less Weekends when nobody could drive.
Lee:	So this goes on all over the world?

Alicia:	Yes. In Africa, people protested the air pollution caused by oil refineries. In Japan, many people ride bicycles that day instead of driving their cars. There are celebrations and protests all over the world on Earth Day!
Lee:	And where is it going to be here in town?
Alicia:	Here at Faber, it's going to be at the student union. There will be exhibits on pollution, we'll plant some trees on campus, and some students will go to other parts of town to help clean up streams and parks.
Lee:	So what are *you* planning to do on Earth Day?
Alicia:	I'm planning to give a speech about pollution. Also, I'm going to carry this sign.
Lee:	*What* does it say? *Save the Earth!* That's great, Alicia. Can I go with you and help? I want to help the environment too.
Alicia:	Sure, Lee. Would *you* like to carry a sign too?
Lee:	Yes, I sure would!

4 **Listening for Specific Information. Page 201.** Listen again. See text for Activity 3.

7 **Listening for Stressed Words. Page 203.** See student text.

PART 2 # Listening Skills

Getting Meaning from Context

1 **Using Context Clues. Page 204.**

Speaker 1

Speaker 1:	In my opinion, it's very dangerous to walk on the streets at night. Someone might steal your money — or even hurt you. The police should do more to stop this problem.

Question 1. What problem is Speaker 1 talking about?

Speaker 1:	Because of crime, I'm afraid. I want to leave this city.

Speaker 2

Speaker 2:	I agree that crime is a problem, but the problem with the air is even bigger. Every day, I look out the window, and the sky is brown and dirty. People shouldn't drive so much. And the factories should run in a cleaner way.

Question 2. What does Speaker 2 think is a bigger problem than crime?

Speaker 2:	Air pollution here is really bad. The city *must* do something to clean up the air.

Speaker 3

Speaker 3:	I agree that crime and air pollution are serious problems. But we shouldn't forget what we have to drink. The rivers are dirty, the city water isn't safe, and I have to buy my water in bottles. Even the rain isn't good for the trees and plants.

Question 3. What does Speaker 3 think is another serious problem?

Speaker 3:   I think crime and air pollution *are* big problems, but water pollution is a big problem too.

Speaker 4

Speaker 4:   I agree with Speakers 1, 2, and 3 that crime and pollution are serious in the city. But to me, just driving from one place to another is the most serious problem. I drive five miles to work, but it takes me half an hour because the traffic is so bad. Every year, there are more cars, trucks, and buses. Then when I go shopping, I have to wait in line for ten or twenty minutes just to pay! There are too few services for too many people.

Question 4. What does Speaker 4 think is the most serious problem in the city?

Speaker 4:   In my opinion, overcrowding is worse than crime and pollution.

Speaker 5

Speaker 5:   It's good to talk about local problems, but I think it's important not to forget the big picture. The cities are only one part of a much bigger problem. We have to find answers to the biggest problem of all - protecting and preserving the earth.

Question 5. What does Speaker 5 think is the biggest problem of all?

Speaker 5:   In other words, we have to understand that problems aren't only in the cities but also in the whole environment.

Listening to Persuasive Messages

3   **Vocabulary Preview. Page 205.** See student text.

4   **Listening for Main Ideas. Page 205.**

Message 1

It takes about 17 mature trees to clean the air of the pollution from one automobile. Give the trees a break on Earth Day and ride your bike or take a free shuttle bus to the Earth Fair in Marquette Park on Monday, April 22. Call 555-1234 for info.

Message 2

What can you do to save the planet on Earth Day? Bring your recyclables to the Earth Fair recycling center at Marquette Park on Monday, April 22, from 10am – 5pm.

Message 3

Less than one out of every quarter *million* slaughtered animals is tested for toxic chemical residues. On Earth Day, eat chemical-free treats at the natural foods area at the Earth Fair in Marquette Park Monday, April 22.

Message 4

A full gallon of water can run out of your faucet in less than sixty seconds! To celebrate Earth Day, turn off the water when you brush your teeth and come to the Earth Fair in Marquette Park on Monday, April 22.

Message 5

One quarter-pound hamburger represents the killing of 55 square feet of rainforest, the loss of ten pounds of topsoil, the use of 650 gallons of water, and the introduction of 500 pounds of carbon dioxide into the atmosphere. Save the planet and eat delicious veggie burgers at the natural foods area at Earth Fair Monday, April 22 at Marquette Park.

5   **Listening for Specific Information. Page 206.** Listen again. See text for Activity 4.

Photo Credits